GYMNASTICS
FOR
MEN

BROWN

PHYSICAL EDUCATION ACTIVITIES SERIES

Consulting Editor:

AILEENE LOCKHART
University of Southern California
Los Angeles, California

Evaluation Materials Editor:

JANE A. MOTT
Smith College
Northampton, Massachusetts

ARCHERY, Wayne C. McKinney
BADMINTON, Margaret Varner
BADMINTON, ADVANCED, Wynn Rogers
BIOPHYSICAL VALUES OF MUSCULAR ACTIVITY, E. C. Davis,
    Gene A. Logan, and Wayne C. McKinney
BOWLING, Joan Martin
CANOEING AND SAILING, Linda Vaughn and Richard Stratton
CIRCUIT TRAINING, Robert P. Sorani
CONDITIONING AND BASIC MOVEMENT CONCEPTS, Jane A. Mott
CONTEMPORARY SQUARE DANCE, Patricia A. Phillips
FENCING, Muriel Bower and Torao Mori
FIELD HOCKEY, Anne Delano
FIGURE SKATING, Marion Proctor
FOLK DANCE, Lois Ellfeldt
GOLF, Virginia L. Nance and E. C. Davis
HANDBALL, Michael Yessis
JUDO, Daeshik Kim
LACROSSE FOR GIRLS AND WOMEN, Anne Delano
BASKETBALL FOR MEN, Glenn Wilkes
GYMNASTICS FOR MEN, A. Bruce Frederick
MODERN DANCE, Esther E. Pease
PHYSICAL AND PHYSIOLOGICAL CONDITIONING FOR MEN, Benjamin Ricci
SKIING, Clayne Jensen and Karl Tucker
SKIN AND SCUBA DIVING, Albert A. Tillman
SOCCER, Richard L. Nelson
SOCIAL DANCE, William F. Pillich
SOFTBALL, Marian E. Kneer and Charles L. McCord
SQUASH RACQUETS, Margaret Varner and Norman Bramall
SWIMMING, Betty J. Vickers and William J. Vincent
TABLE TENNIS, Margaret Varner and J. R. Harrison
TAP DANCE, Barbara Nash
TENNIS, Joan Johnson and Paul Xanthos
TENNIS, ADVANCED, Chet Murphy
TRACK AND FIELD, Kenneth E. Foreman and Virginia L. Husted
TRAMPOLINING, Jeff T. Hennessy
VOLLEYBALL, Glen H. Egstrom and Frances Schaafsma
WEIGHT TRAINING, Philip J. Rasch
BASKETBALL FOR WOMEN, Frances Schaafsma
GYMNASTICS FOR WOMEN, A. Bruce Frederick
WRESTLING, Arnold Umbach and Warren R. Johnson

PHYSICAL EDUCATION
ACTIVITIES SERIES

GYMNASTICS
FOR
MEN

A. BRUCE FREDERICK

Wisconsin State University
Superior, Wisconsin

WM. C. BROWN COMPANY PUBLISHERS
DUBUQUE, IOWA

Preface

There are many ways to think about and describe the world of gymnastics. Gymnastics may be politically or nationalistically inspired. Medical gymnastics may be prescribed for those who may benefit from its therapeutic effects. Professional gymnasts are found under the "Big Top."

Unique kinds of gymnastics have also been developed for girls, housewives, boys and men. Oldsters and youngsters, sometimes together, take part in gymnastic programs of all types in Europe and also in those isolated corners of our own country where the influence of immigrants has produced gymnastics clubs such as the Turners, the Sokols and the Falcons. It's amazing, however, that the programs of these groups have not had a more lasting influence on American culture. The Turners are generally credited with the first programs of physical education in this country, and many Turner clubs have celebrated centennials.

Competitive gymnastics for boys and men, although growing, is not well known nor widely practiced in English-speaking countries. The Olympic stature accorded this sport, however, does indicate that the world respects a gymnast. Many foreign physical educators consider gymnastics the foundation or the base for all sports and have suggested that their countrymen have scored high on tests of physical fitness because of the emphasis placed on gymnastic training.

The reason you are reading this book probably has little to do with any of the discussion above. Your gymnastic goals are probably more closely related to a personal level of skill. "How much gymnastics can I learn?" "How can I start?"

The purpose of this book is one of introduction. The hope is that you will get off on the right track. It cannot replace the years of accomplishment you might have experienced if gymnastics were an important part of our culture. It isn't. It should be!

PREFACE

Self-evaluation questions pertaining to both knowledge and skill are included in these pages. These should give the reader examples of the kinds of understandings he should be acquiring and the kinds of abilities he should be developing in his mastery of gymnastics techniques. Respond to the questions carefully and devise additional ones to stimulate your learning.

The best way to enter the gymnast's world is through active participation. You have already mastered a portion of the content since, in a broad sense, anyone who moves is a potential gymnast. When that movement has some special meaning; when it is exhilarating; when it increases human efficiency; when it is elegant or when it is loved, then that is gymnastics.

A. B. Frederick

DEDICATION

To my parents who provided the spark and L. B.
who keeps it burning.

Contents

An original drawing by Ivan Foster, Oak Grove Schools, Elsmere, Delaware.

Preparation
for Gymnastics

Your initiation to gymnastics requires both understanding and patience. Your potential can be self-judged below as you participate in a gymnastic "physical" and ponder mechanical principles. Since the principles of mechanics are combined with action, they will take on some personal meaning as you solve the problems suggested. In the final portion of the chapter there are a few suggestions on dress.

Thus your preparation consists of what you bring (your body and your equipment) and what you learn about basic gymnastic mechanics.

YOUR PERFORMERS: THE MUSCLES

Performance is the simultaneous participation of mind and body in any body movement. The performers of the mind-body organism known as man are muscles. When they are properly conditioned and combined in movement, progress in gymnastics is accelerated.

Muscles can do two things. They get shorter (contract) or simply do nothing (relax). A relaxed muscle may be stretched or lengthened by the action of other muscles. Each function of muscle must extend to reasonable limits if early success in gymnastics is desired. In gymnastics we characteristically speak of strength and flexibility. The former is a function of muscle contraction; the latter is a function of stretched muscles and joint action (where two bones are connected).

The Olympic gymnast typically has both strength and flexibility. He is strong enough to hold an iron cross for three seconds (Figure 1-1) and flexible enough to do splits (Figure 1-2). You will find that your first gymnastic goals are intimately bound up with the development of appropriate strength and flexibility.

Men are of three basic types: skinny, fat and muscular. Each kind of man has unique problems. The thin man is usually least flexible of the three. The overweight person carries a load which is very often incompatible with even fundamental gymnastic work. To be successful he must rid himself of this extra burden. In gymnastics, "skinny" will have some advantage over "fat."

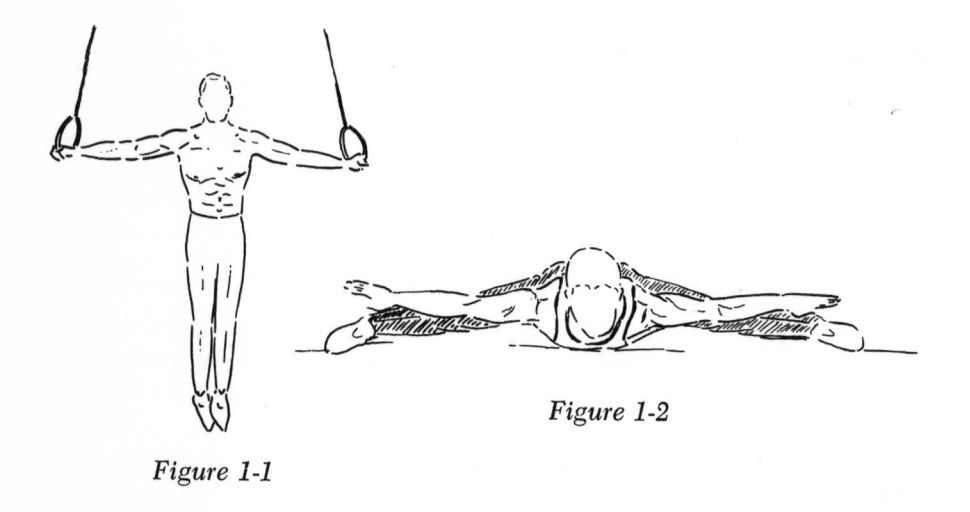

Figure 1-2

Figure 1-1

The muscular fellow is somewhat better off than his two friends, but he often experiences a combination of flexibility and weight problems. The stocky football lineman may have difficulty lifting his weight gymnastically; the weight lifter may have trouble with range of movement.

Fortunately, most boys and men are neither skinny nor fat. Neither can the majority of men be described as muscular. We must, however, accept what we are and then try to do something about it. Gymnastics offers no mystical or quick path to physical fitness. It does offer a great motor motivator since the goal is performance rather than health, fitness or muscle building. A handstand is its own reward. It is gymnastic. Could you say the same for push-ups? Probably not!

STRENGTH

You must have enough strength to pull yourself up on things, support your weight in balance or in swing and develop a grip to hold on to apparatus. Your protective abdominal wall ("stomach muscles") should be tight and flat. It plays a key role.

1. ARMS AND SHOULDERS—Since the arms and shoulders are often called on to lift and support the body in gymnastics, we give them first billing here. The push-up and pull-up are general standards of measurement for arm performance. If you cannot do at least one of each you are in trouble! Let us assume you have some problem at this point. To train toward the performance of a single pull-up, start by having someone push you up to a bent arm hang (Figure 1-3). From this position come down as slowly as you can and fight the tendency to drop. While coming down you use the same muscles it takes to pull up. In time such training usually results in the ability to do one or more pull-ups.

The "coming down slowly" principle also applies to the push-up. In Figure 1-4 the performer lets himself down slowly and attempts to touch his nose to the floor in *front* of his hands with slightly bent hips. By bending slightly at the hips you may avoid the common "swayback" push-up which does not tax the muscles to a sufficient degree to result in improvement. Thus the "let down" technique is a form of negative exercise in which gravity helps rather than hinders performance.

Pretty soon you may expect to see muscle definition that is characteristic in the gymnast's arm and is depicted in Figure 1-5. Tone up in front of a mirror and look for the ridges, bulges and valleys that are shown in the drawing.

Heaving up against a bar (Figure 1-6) until tired should result in increased strength and endurance in the arms and shoulders.

2. ABDOMEN—The traditional exercise for abdominal muscles is the sit-up. It can be performed in many ways, but the curl down shown in Figure 1-7 is one of the best. Again, emphasis is on slowness. By the time you reach position 4 you may be tempted to collapse. Try to hold firm at this point and continue slowly to your back. Firm abdominal mucles are shown in Figure 1-8.

3. GRIP—You can test your grip with an ordinary bathroom scale. Simply pick it up with one hand on either side (thumb on top; fingers on the bottom), then squeeze. You should be able to register 110 pounds or more.

Can you hang on a bar for one minute? If you need to increase your strength in this area, habitually squeezing a small, rubber, sponge ball will be helpful.

4. LEGS—The gymnast's legs are important even when he is not using them for support. In a handstand, for example, they must be toned up so that balance can be controlled. The tumbler, vaulter and trampolinist need to have and develop leg strength.

3

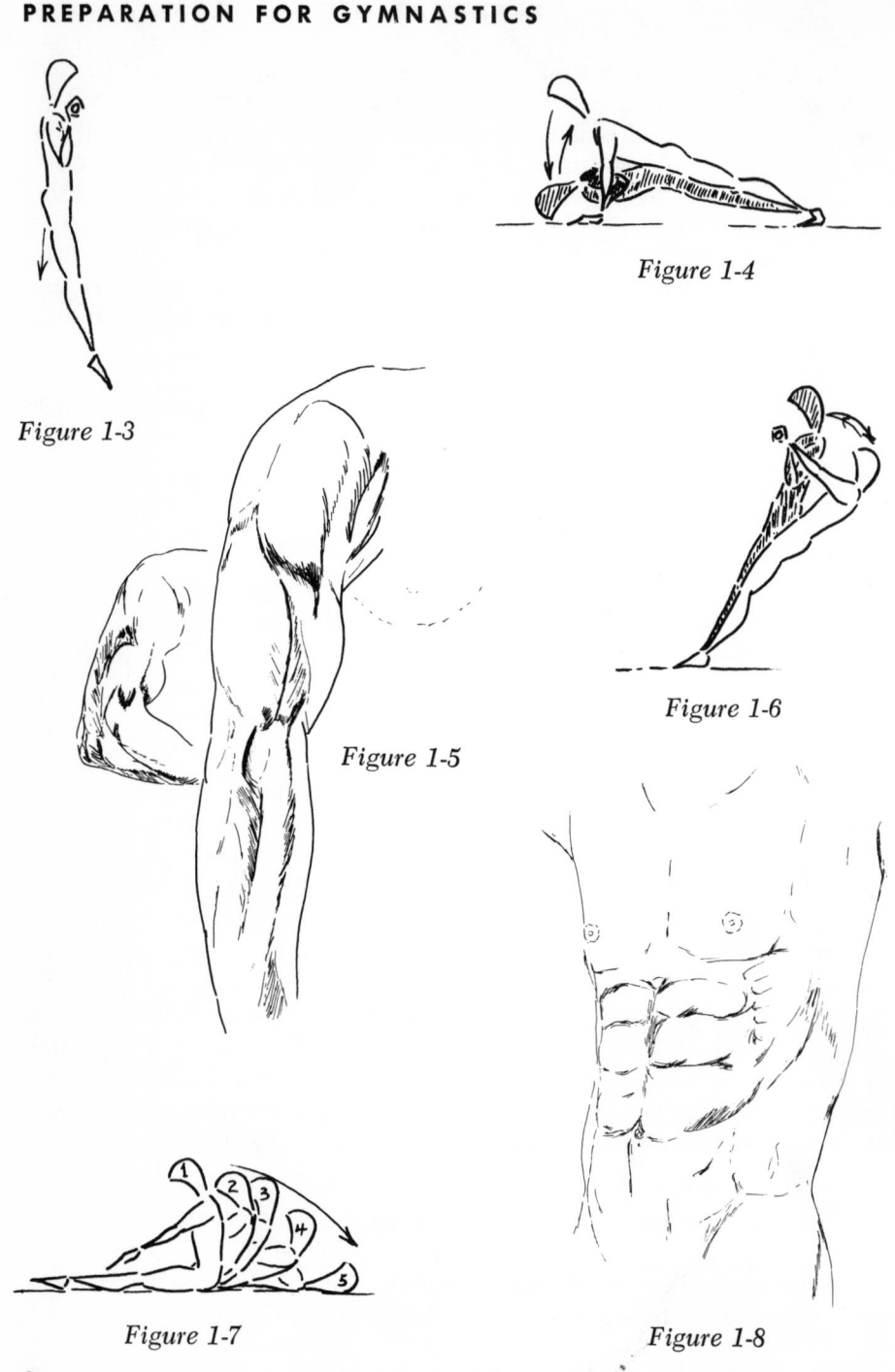

Figure 1-3

Figure 1-4

Figure 1-5

Figure 1-6

Figure 1-7

Figure 1-8

Running is an excellent way to keep the legs in shape. Gentle, rhythmic bounding on a trampoline is also a good practice. Both of these activities also tax the heart and lungs. In Kunzle's excellent book[1] we find rope skipping highly recommended. He also recommends the exercise shown in Figure 1-9. Notice the leg extension when the body is airborne.

A firmed-up leg is shown in Figure 1-10. By observation and feeling definition, you will be cultivating habitual control of your muscles.

5. BACK—In gymnastics we normally think of the back in terms of flexibility rather than strength. Most of your back muscles will firm, however, when you try to hold the position shown in Figure 1-11.

FLEXIBILITY

In gymnastics you will extend your range of movement by stretching your muscles. Muscles which are not stretched properly prevent extension of the arms and legs by constricting the action of the joints. The backbending action of the bridge shown in Figure 1-12 (Position 2 or 3) is simply impossible when the spine and vertebral joints are constricted by inflexible muscles.

1. BACK—Three general types of backs are shown in Figure 1-12. The stiff back (1) is very common in boys who are untrained in gymnastics. Only daily stretching will result in improvement. This practice must become habitual.

If your back is extremely loose (3) you have an acrobatic back. Fortunately, not many men are this flexible and this should *not* be one of your goals.

The gymnastic back (2) is the one you want. It is the happy medium, allowing a majority of movements requiring back suppleness.

2. SHOULDER—If your back is stiff, stretching through the shoulder joints will serve a dual purpose. Fairly loose shoulders make up somewhat for a relatively stiff back. Practice the exercises shown in Figures 1-13 and 1-14 and find a partner to work with you.

3. TOE POINTING—Pointing the toes extends the range of movement at the ankle joint. Toe point helps arrange the leg into one unit of length which in turn is easier to control. Toe point, combined with the upper and lower leg in extension, provides you with a single, swinging unit that can be used very effectively in gymnastics. It is easier to control one piece than three!

The supple movement shown in Figure 1-15 is often used as a warm-up exercise. Notice that you start with the top of the foot down. Practice with

[1]G. Kunzle, and B. W. Thomas, *Olympic Gymnastics—Freestanding* (Olympic Gymnastic Series, Vol. I), London: James Barrie Publishers, 1956, pp. 25-26.

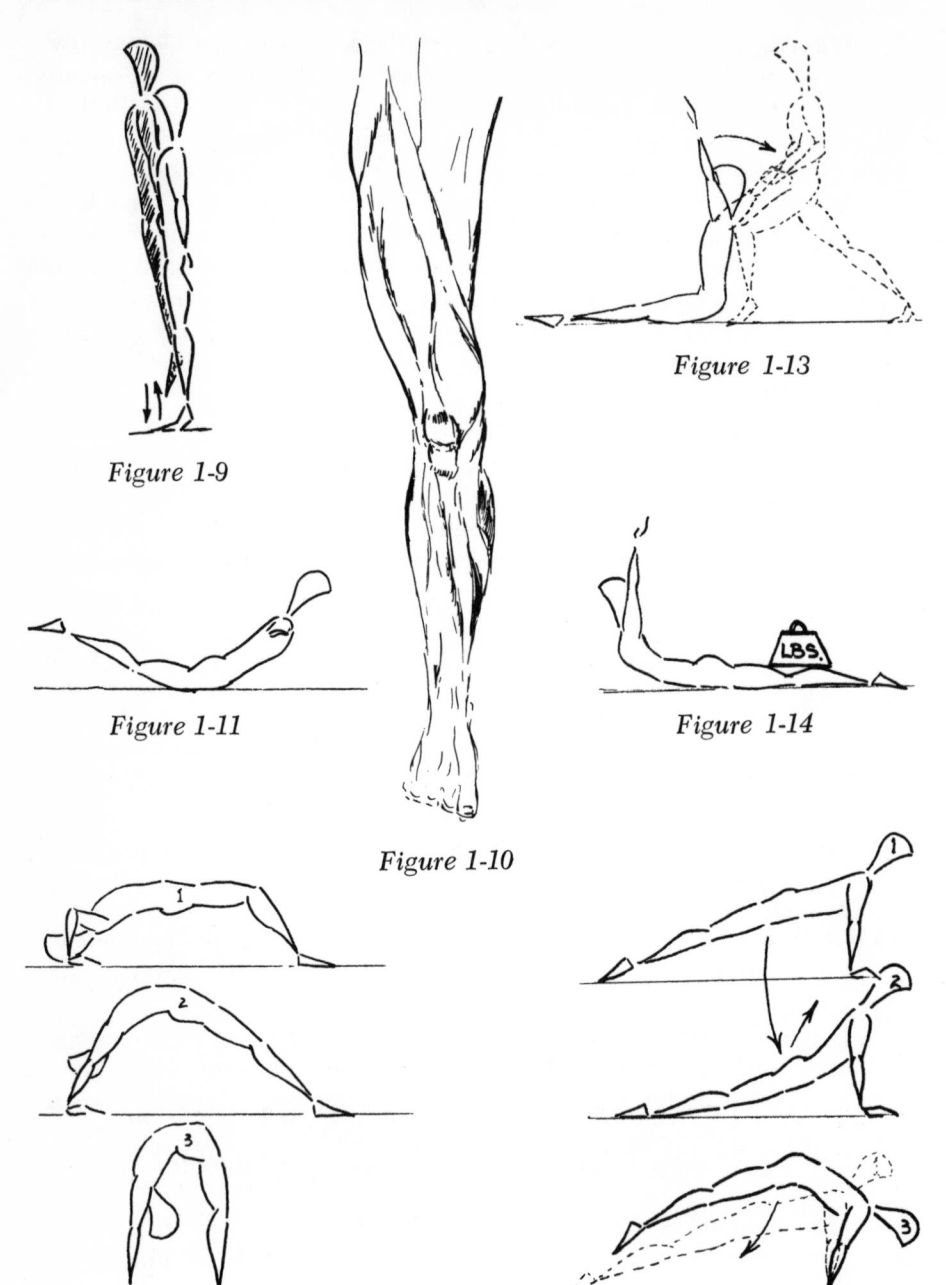

Figure 1-9

Figure 1-13

Figure 1-11

Figure 1-14

Figure 1-10

Figure 1-12

Figure 1-15

care. Many beginners tend to stub their toes. Make sure your practice area is well padded. Once you gain control it will not be difficult to practice on a hard surface such as a gymnasium floor

4. HAMSTRINGS—Whenever you straighten your leg, your hamstrings (located behind your thigh) stretch. If they do not stretch properly, you will not achieve good leg extension. If you can touch your fingers to the floor comfortably with no bend at the knees, your hamstrings are stretching normally, If you are not flexible in the hamstrings, daily practice is again required. (See Figure 1-16.)

Figure 1-16

Stretch slowly to the point of discomfort. Never bounce. A little pain indicates that you are stretching and that is your goal.

Splits are also very commonly performed by the gymnast to stretch the hamstrings. There are two kinds: front and back splits (Figure 1-17) and side splits (Figure 1-18). As you practice, remember to proceed slowly and steadily to the point of pain. Splits are *not* naturally done by most untrained boys and men. Practice them daily. Do not bounce!

Figure 1-17   *Figure 1-18*

In the author's experience, flexibility training has generally provided his gymnasts a greater measure of related success than strength exercises. With beginners, there is little question about the a priori status of flexibility.

CHAIR GYMNASTICS (FIGURE 1-19, NUMERALS 1 TO 46)

Thus far, the exercises we have presented are generally classified as calisthenics. They are not particularly fun to do albeit necessary. Gymnastic's appeal is quickly discovered by virtue of gymnastic not calisthenic performance. Chair gymnastics is simply a more pleasing way to combine most of the elements above into one complete routine.

Performed daily, you will begin to understand your weaknesses. Smooth transition from one part of the routine to another will acquaint you with

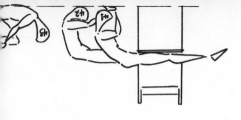

Figure 1-19

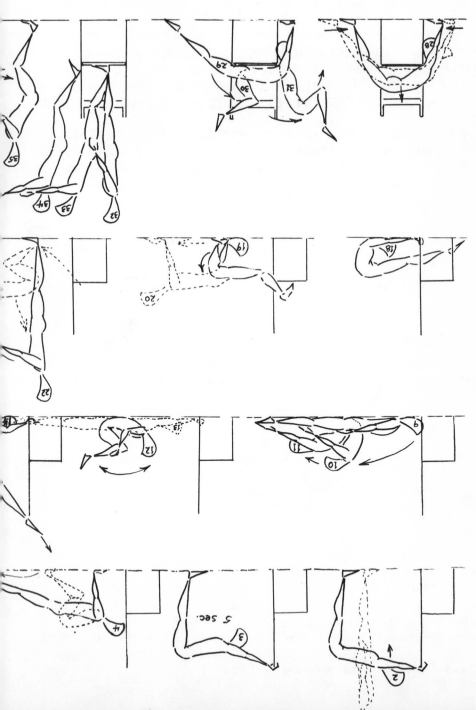

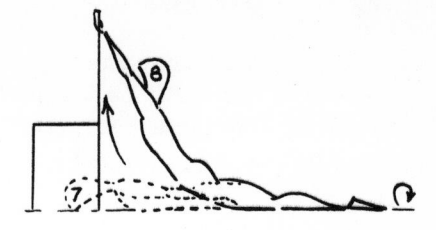
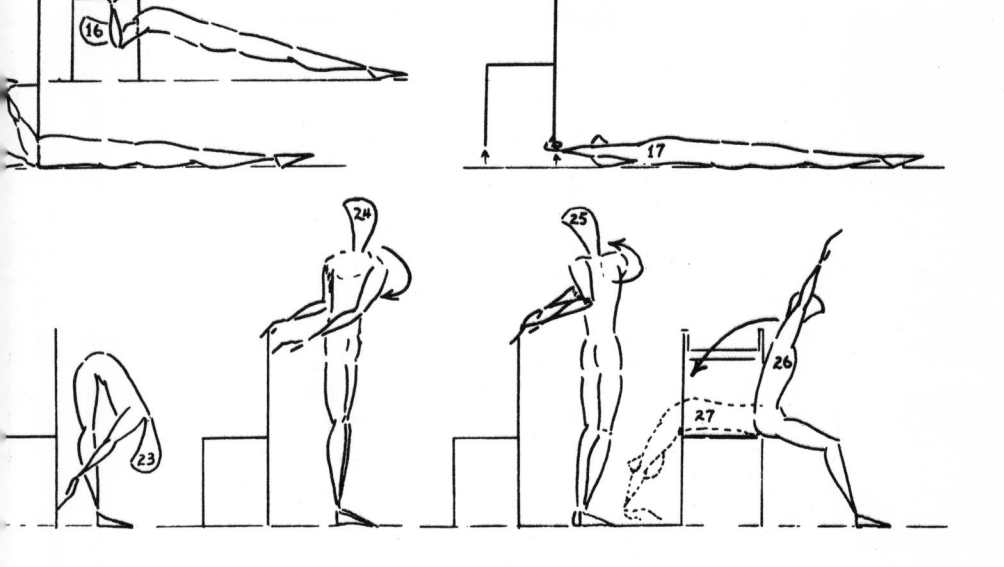
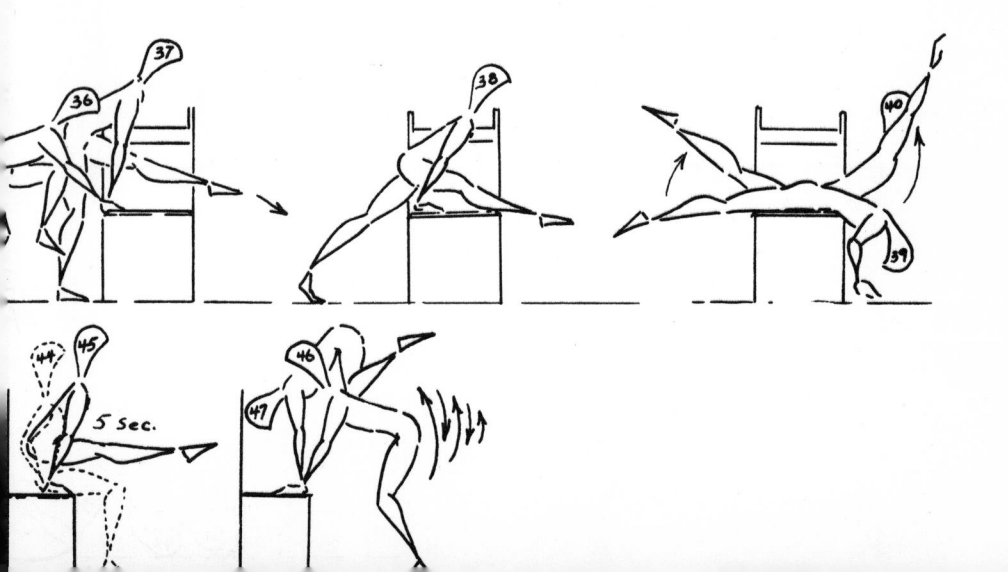

elements of gymnastic continuity. Add things; be creative. But do not eliminate. Use a musical background if you like.

The first few times you perform, have a partner read the directions to you. Then do the same for him. Learning to work with a partner has many benefits.

Stand in back of chair as shown (2), grasping top edge with hands. Press shoulders down for 5 seconds (3). Drop hands to floor and squat (4). Extend legs to push-up position. Lower slowly to (5) with nose touching floor in front of hands. Hold for 5 seconds. Lift hips slowly as high as possible without moving hands or feet (6). Lower slowly to floor (7). Reach for top of chair (8). Reach up and return to floor three times. Turn over to your back (9). Curl up through (10) to (11) and return to position (9). Keep your hands in contact with your legs at all times. Repeat the curl-ups two more times. Tuck up (12), and roll gently back and forth until rested. Reach for lower legs of chair and stretch out (13). Arms are fully extended. Roll up (14) and stretch to get your feet higher than the chair. Try not to touch the chair with your body. Do at least two extensions in a row without touching the chair. Slide under the chair (15). Pull up and heave the chest upward five times (16). Slide out to (17). Try to lift the chair from the floor with straight arms. Lower chair. Pike (no bend at knees) roll backward to pretzel bend (18). Hold position briefly and attempt to firm up and extend the legs. Placing your hands as shown, hook your toes around seat of chair and curl out (19 to 20). Move to squat stand (21) and stand up (22). Bend forward with straight legs and attempt to touch the chair as low as possible (23). Repeat two more times. Now perform the turn and touch (24 and 25). Turn twenty times without moving your feet; try to keep your legs straight. On the last turn, place the chair and sit in it as shown in (26). Sit on the edge. Slowly stretch back to (27) and place your hands on the floor as shown. Fingers point toward the feet. Extend the abdomen upward, weight on hands and feet (28). Clear the chair and return at least three times, then turn over the seat (back roll) as seen in (29-30). Your buddy should be in a position to grasp your hips as you turn over to your feet. Step up on the chair (32). Jump to the floor with control (32-35). Turn and mount the chair once again. Repeat jumping until you land in control three times (take up the shock in your knees and ankles and hold the landing position without moving your feet). As you progress in following days, try to jump higher. If you lose control, you are jumping too high. Place your hands on the edge of the seat (36) and thread the needle with one of your legs (37). Straighten both legs and move forward to (38). Repeat with the other leg. Lie on the chair (39) and arch up slowly to (40). Repeat this movement two more times and hold the arch for five seconds on each try. Roll forward (forward roll) as in (41-43). Stand up. Sit on chair (44). Push up to L and hold for 5 seconds (45). Place hands on chair (46). Support jump to (47). Repeat until tired. You're done!

GYMNASTIC THEORY

This section is devoted to gymnastic theory. As you read, try to solve all the problems posed immediately after they are given.

PROBLEM 1—Just for "openers," can you think of one movement performed by man (gymnastic or not) that is not angular (circular) in part?

Remember that your body is constructed around and between a group of bones (skeleton). Where two bones come together, a joint is formed and the range of motion at any joint can be understood in terms of degrees. (In Figure 1-20, the forearm represents a moving radius. How many degrees has it moved?) You will find no linear movements described in this book, but it would be inaccurate to say there are none. When man provides the force for his own movement, that movement *is* angular in whole or in part. The direction the body travels might be relatively straight (running), but just think of all the joints which are in motion in running.

Definitions—Rather than memorizing the following definitions, try to apply them. Imagine or perform some movement which incorporates each definition. We recommend Dyson's excellent book[2] if you feel inspired to pursue some of the definitions a bit further.

> *Gravity*—That force which pulls us toward the center of the earth.
>
> *Center of Gravity*—Let us say it another way, "Center of weight." All matter has weight. In regular solids, such as cubes and cones, the center of weight is easy to find. Their shapes do not change. Man's shape is irregular and he may change his shape at will. Therefore, his center of weight is relative. At attention (See Figure 1-21) his center of weight (center of gravity or simply C. G.) is slightly above the hips and equidistant from the front and back of the body.
>
> *Axes*—An axis is a theoretical line around which a mass of weight rotates. We have three primary axes. Each passes through the C. G. of the body. In Figure 1-21 A is the long axis of the body. It runs from head to feet. B is the hip-to-hip axis or gymnastic axis since so many gymnastic movements are involved with it. The cartwheeling axis is C. Absolute rotation about these axes only occurs when you are in the air so for most movements on the ground they are merely points of reference. When you make contact with the ground, the body rotates around parts in contact with the ground.

PROBLEM 2—In Figure 1-22 the figures represent rotations which are more or less representative of axes A, B and C. Identify each axis. Only one figure represents a true rotation around a primary body axis. Which?

> *Moments*—No, we do *not* refer to time when we use the term *moment* here. Think of a moment as a broomstick. If you carefully arrange the straws of the broom, it will stand up by itself. It is in balance. But the instant (moment) it becomes unbalanced, it begins to fall and a "moment" or rotation is created. In Figure 1-23 the gymnast is falling out of balance. A force is responsible for this (moment of force). An equal force must be overcome (moment of inertia). The "moment arm" is the distance from the point of rotation of the moment to the C. G.

PROBLEM 3—In Figure 1-23, which letter represents the moment arm? Can you also identify or supply an explanation for the things represented by the other letters in Figure 1-23?

---

[2]Geoffrey Dyson, *The Mechanics of Athletics* 3rd ed., London: University of London Press, 1964.

Figure 1-20

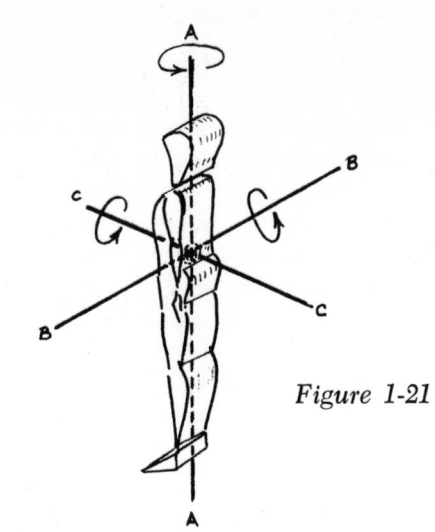

Figure 1-21

Figure 1-22

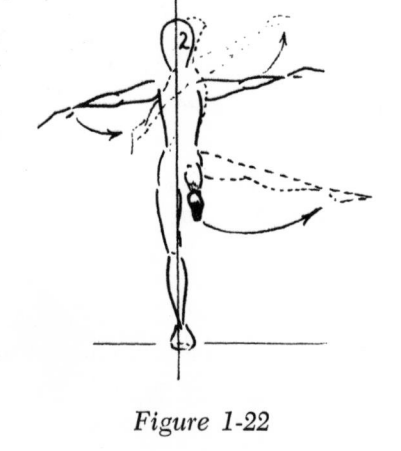

Figure 1-22

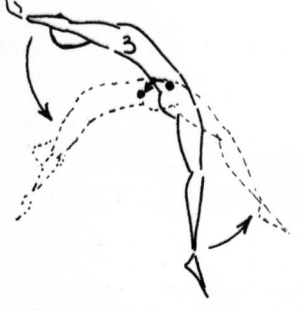

Figure 1-22

NEWTON'S LAWS OF MOTION

Law I   (*The Law of Inertia*)—In any movement the body becomes active because of some force such as gravity. Once in motion, your body tends to keep moving until another force such as friction restricts the action. The tendency to stay in motion or at rest is known as inertia.

Law II   (*The Law of Momentum*)—Imagine you are moving at a given rate of speed (running e. g.). While running, a gust of wind suddenly hits your back and you run faster or accelerate. Knowledge of this law helps explain good spotting. For example, it is much more efficient to give assistance to a performer while he is accelerating. In jumping from the floor, therefore, you would provide assistance on the way up not on the way down.

Law III   (*The Law of Action-Reaction,* or Jet Propulsion)—For every action there is an equal and opposite reaction. Every movement has an action-reaction phase; the more action, the more reaction.

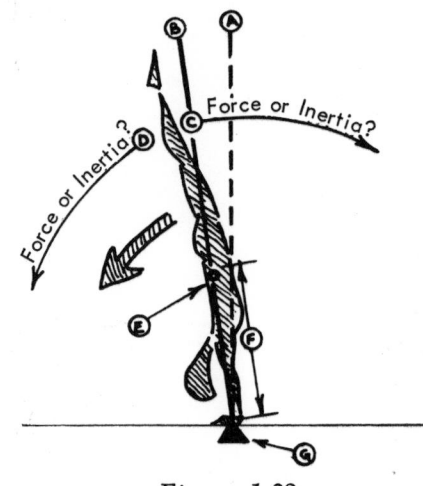

Figure 1-23

PROBLEM 4—Try to jump up without first going down. Can you? Why or why not?

     Levers—Understanding leverage will help you understand something about your unique construction. Bones do not rotate at joints by themselves. They are moved by muscle. Therefore, bones are levers; joints represent points of rotation (fulcra), and force is provided by muscle. Levers are of three classes: first, second and third.

     1st Class Levers (See-saw lever)—Diagrams of levers are found in Figure 1-24. There are not many 1st class levers in the body. One of the most obvious is found in the forward-backward action of the head. Notice that this is the only lever where the fulcrum (represented by little triangles) falls between the force arm (F) and the

13

The gymnast is performing a sit-up. The muscle (in black) is getting shorter. Can you draw in appropriate symbols to show the type of lever shown in the action?

Evaluation Questions

LEVERAGE

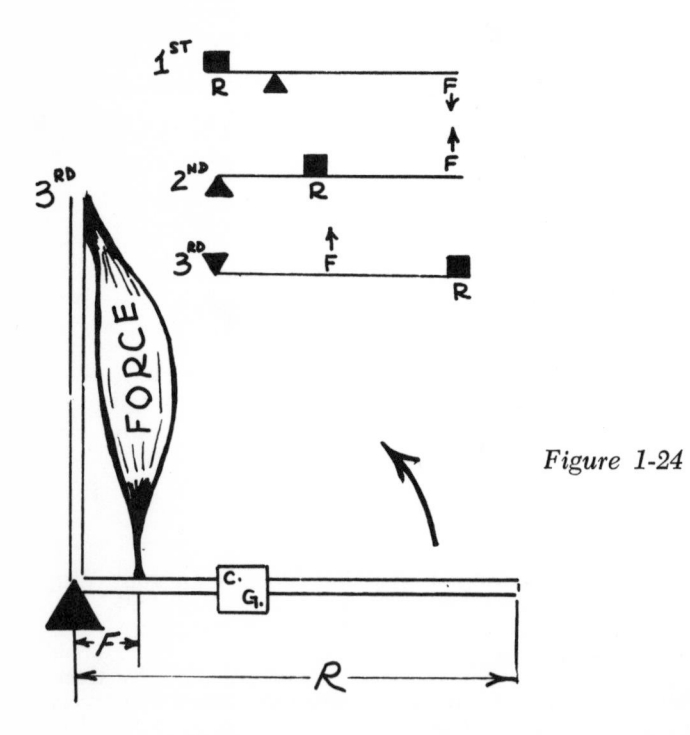

Figure 1-24

resistance arm (R). The measurement of either the force arm or the resistance arm is taken from the fulcrum to the point on the lever where the F or R is applied.

2nd *Class Levers* (Wheel barrow lever)—This class of levers has a longer force arm with the fulcrum at one end. There are few, if

Diagram A:

LEVERAGE

any, of this class in the human mechanism. We are not built for strength!

3rd *Class Levers* (The human lever)—Our bodies are loaded with third class levers. A typical model is shown in Figure 1-24. To be efficient in movement we should take advantage of speed and range because we *are* built for this kind of action. Why? Take a look! The force arm is so much smaller than the resistance arm. In gymnastics, therefore, we encourage stretching; we encourage toe point and flexibility. Why? Simply because it makes you longer. When you are at your longest, you squeeze out the most from your unique lever system.

Balance—There are six general principles:

1. Maintain the C. G. over the base of support.
2. The greater the base, the more stable the balance.
3. For better stability, enlarge your base in the direction of a force. See Figure 1-26.
4. For each shift of weight in one direction, there must be an appropriate shift in the opposite direction.
5. When the C. G. is raised, stability decreases. Compare standing on one foot with standing on the ball of the same foot.
6. Rotary action increases stability. In gymnastics we immediately think of double leg circles on the side horse. You are familiar with the stability and balance of a spinning top.

PROBLEM 5—Stand with your heels against a wall and try to touch the floor. What happens, and why?

PROBLEM 6—Sit on a chair. Now stand up. Explain how you are able to stand in terms of what you have learned above.

Conservation of Angular Momentum—In gymnastic circling movements like the giant swing, hip circle and knee circle we find that performance

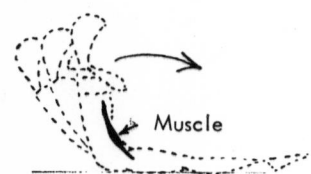

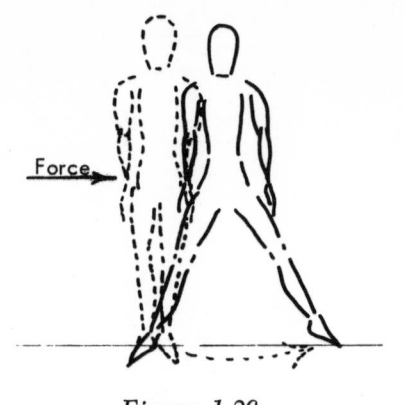

Figure 1-25

Figure 1-26

is related to the principle described here. Circles are of two general kinds: long axis circles (e.g. ice skaters spin) and hip-to-hip axis circles. In the latter the path of the circle is perpendicular to the floor. All bar circles are in this category. In Figure 1-27 you see diagrams of the giant swing and the knee circle. Both are performed on a bar. The dotted circles are true circles. The solid lines represent the ovoid path of the C. G. as the gymnast performs. Gymnastic circles are not actual

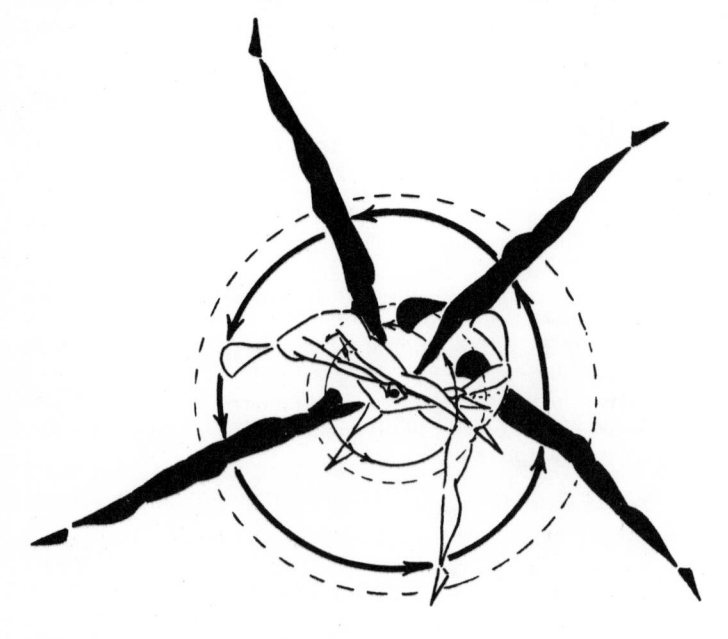

Figure 1-27

circles. If the C. G. were to remain a constant distance from the bar, the circle could *not* be completed! The primary reason for this is friction. We can not eliminate friction and we can't vary the force of gravity since it is constant. What we can and must do is change the shape of the body. In bar circles there are two main phases: going down and coming up. Gravity works with us on the way down; it works against us on the way up. Maximum angular momentum is obtained by making the body long on the way down and shorter on the way up. By shortening the body or decreasing the distance of the C. G. from the bar we conserve momentum by accelerating at a time when we really need it. Notice how the gymnasts in Figure 1-27 accomplish both phases. How does the spinning ice skater go faster? The same principle applies. Extend on the way down; shorten on the way up. In this respect all gymnastic "circles" are the same.

PERSONAL EQUIPMENT

All sports require unique, personal equipment. For some activities the equipment and gear is protective; for others the goal is comfort and range of movement.

As a gymnastic beginner you will learn to wear special apparel that is both protective and comfortable. You should eliminate heavy tennis or basketball shoes (barefeet are okay) and wear clothing which is loose fitting and yet needs no constant tucking in.

SLIPPERS—Gymnastic slippers (Figure 1-28) are commonly made of canvas or light leather. They provide comfortable and seemingly weightless covering for the feet. Soles of the slippers may be rubber or felt depending on the amount of friction desired. Rubber soles are best for beginners. If your local sporting goods store has none in stock they can order them for you. Some dancing schools also keep a supply of gymnastic slippers. Stockings alone may be dangerous since you are apt to slip and because you cannot run properly when they are worn without slippers or shoes. Bare feet are preferable.

Figure 1-28

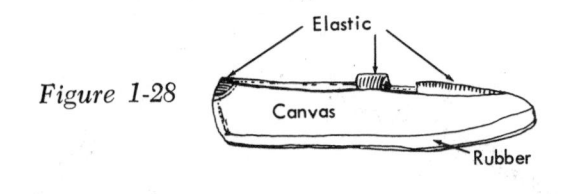

SHIRT—A "T" shirt is commonly used by the beginner. There are gymnastic shirts available known as step-ins or a male leotard. (Don't feel bad, the leotard was named after a famous *male* circus performer by the same name.) The step-in has the advantage of not pulling out for there is no "tail" to get in the way. Sweatshirts provide protection for your first experiences on parallel bars, which can be hard on the soft skin under the upper arms. Sweatshirts also prevent abrasions in beginning work on the trampoline.

SHORTS—Most gym shorts and bathing suits may be worn by the beginner, but beginning work on the trampoline is most comfortable when knees are protected by sweat pants or light cotton trousers. Some excellent two-way stretch warm-up suits are available, consisting of tights and jacket which are suitable for all varieties of gymnastic work.

FORM PANTS—These pants are constructed especially for the competitor. Modern gymnastic trousers are made of stretch nylon with an elastic band joining the cuffs at the bottom of each leg. They also have sewn in creases. Their function is both practical and protective, and they give a trim aesthetic appearance.

Form pants are especially valuable in the beginning stages of side horse work. The legs are able to slide across the leather surface of the horse, and abrasions and hair pulling are avoided. Since they stretch and fit the legs rather closely, they are not apt to become entangled on the parallel bars or the high bar.

HAND PROTECTION—Stay with a gymnast long enough and you will shortly be introduced to a white powder known as "mag" (magnesium carbonate). It is available in most drugstores in a block, and there are powdered and aerosol forms. Since the powder is absorbent, it helps keep the hands dry and reduces the incidence of blisters.

Apparatus gymnastics is similar to other hard work affecting the hands such as work with picks and shovels. Friction is always a factor. Therefore the gymnast works carefully and never lets his hands get to the burning, blistering stage. A torn blister, or rip takes time to heal properly. Since the tender layer of skin beneath the top layer is exposed, working with rips is painful and should be avoided. Soaking the hands daily and applying a first aid cream promotes healing and prevents edges of the rip from becoming hard.

As you advance in gymnastics you should get used to wearing hand grips or lampwicks. (See Figure 1-29.) When grips are used in combination with mag there is no need for the hands to rip if they are not overtaxed. Since grips are always a bit uncomfortable at first, get used to them as a beginner even though they are not absolutely necessary.

Remove rings from your hands while performing on the apparatus. In fact, remove all kinds of jewelry including identification bracelets and religious medals. Rings promote blisters and rips because they cause the skin beneath them to bunch up, thus causing more friction and pressure.

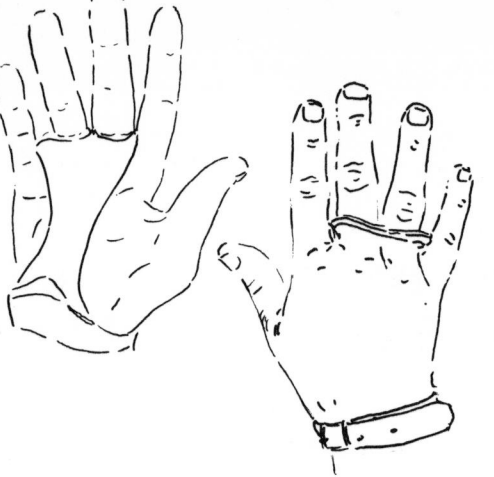

Figure 1-29

SUPPORTER—As in all vigorous activities make it a habit to wear an athletic supporter. Always include the supporter as a regular part of your uniform regardless of what you intend to do.

2

Skills for Everyone— Gymnastics' Big Five

An all-around gymnast is one who involves himself in every gymnastic event. The program in gymnastics is such that overspecialization can result in development that could hardly be described as good physical education. The gymnasts who are skilled enough for Olympic competition do not specialize; they *must* be all-around performers. This does not happen by accident! You will like some parts of the whole better than others, but it is important that you are exposed to and practice in every gymnastic department.

Due to limitations of space, the author has elected to acquaint you with the raw materials for gymnastic development. In this chapter, rather than finding subheadings for each gymnastic event, you will learn about gymnastics' "Big Five."

The "Big Five" are symbolized in Figure 2-1. The model represents all of gymnastics from the elementary to the advanced level. Each of the "Big Five" (swing, balance, flexibility, strength and agility) has a unique place on the model. See if you can identify each in terms of their geometric symbols. Try to have an idea about the "why?" of this arrangement before you read further.

The words, "who can swing can do gymnastics" are those of Helmut Bantz, a respected German teacher and former Olympian. His *Turnmethodik*[3] and philosophy gave inspiration for the organization of this chapter. The contents are fundamental and conducive to all-around work. When appropriate, apparatus exercise is introduced as a part of a unique aspect of the "Big Five."

---

[3]Helmut Bantz and Adalbert Dickhut, *Turnmethodik*, Frankfurt/Main, Germany: Wilhelm Limpert Verlag, 1959. Note: This publisher is the source of many excellent gymnastic books including the popular *Wer Kann?* ("Who Can?").

In its widest interpretation, *swing* refers to gymnastic movement in general, cutting through all areas of the "Big Five." The basis for this idea is found in the anatomy of man. Man moves by a system of levers, mostly lever class three, which has the advantage of speed and range rather than force. When we extend the range of our bodies, we not only swing better, we move efficiently as well. In the modern, gymnastic idiom, *amplitude* often describes desirable form. It is the extreme *range* of a *fluctuating* (man can change his shape) quality. In our model, the swing triangle cuts through or touches all components of the "Big Five," and if you concentrate you will see an arrow pointing to the little swinger at the apex, thus symbolizing the importance of swing.

Balance may be thought of as achieving nonmovement (this is not accurate physiologically), but in all actions of the body there is dynamic balance as well. Balance has a central location in the model. It is the heart of gymnstics: static and dynamic. The gray semicircle symbolizing balance shades significant portions of the other members. Balance even goes beyond the limits of the model and thus accounts for times when the body is completely at rest (for example, in deep sleep).

At the extreme left and right sides of the model is a rectangle representing the outriggers of gymnastics: strength and flexibility. The rectangles are identical in size, and their major portions lie within the swing triangle. They represent fundamental swinging movements basically dependent on either strength or flexibility or both.

Outside the triangle, portions of the rectangles represent purer forms of strength and flexibility. The L cross on the rings takes unusual strength; the flexibility of a German giant swing is also an extreme.

Figure 2-1

Can you explain the content of the model shown in Figure 2-1 and the logic of the arrangement of the symbols?

Evaluation Questions

Most gymnastic movements require combinations of either flexibility-swing-balance or strength-swing-balance, and such intersections and over-lappings are evident on the model.

The rectangular base of the model represents the fifth element: agility. The symbolic figure at the base of the model is in this category. By agility we simply mean traveling over something. This includes running, hopping, jumping and leaping. It includes that most fundamental of all forms of gymnastics: tumbling. Basic movement, tumbling and traditional vaulting over the horse and other apparatus are massed together and called agility collectively for purposes of the "Big Five." Since these activities are funda-mental to all gymnastics, agility thus becomes the base of the model. These are the elements you will be taught first and thoroughly before you proceed to supportive work on apparatus.

The remaining sections of this chapter are devoted to a beginner's involvement with the "Big Five."

SWING

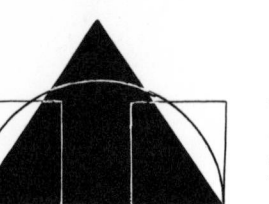

Putting your third class lever mechanism to work gymnastically requires that you become thoroughly familiar with swing in the forms of kipping, casting, swinging, circling and kicking.

1. FLOOR KIPPING—Folding and unfolding the body at the hips is a loose description of kipping. Kipping action, resulting in elevation of the C. G., is probably the most common of typically identifiable gymnastic movements. Kips are some-

times masked by other names such as "Peachbasket," but they are still basically kips. Before we begin work with typical beginner's kips, there are a few fundamentals to master.

A. *Rolling* (Figure 2-2)—Lie down, then simply grasp your shins (tuck) and roll back and forth. Try to roll forward and backward rather than from side to side. Once your roll is controlled, release your shins as you roll to your upper back and place your hands as shown in Figure 2-3 each time you roll back.

B. *Piked Rolling* (Figure 2-3)—This is the same rolling action described in A above, but the legs are fully extended and the body rolls piked. Have someone observe your roll to see if the legs are really straight. Reach forward as you roll up.

C. *Candle* (Figure 2-4)—Rolling back to a candle shape will help you feel the full extension necessary to perform quality kipping action.

D. *Balance Point* (Figure 2-5A)—Roll back and see if you can *hold* this position. It is an excellent orientation exercise for many similar positions you will be asked to perform later on.

Thus far you have not done a kip. You have simply prepared for kipping actions which follow. If you are having trouble keeping your legs straight (no bend at the knees) your kipping actions will be affected accordingly.

E. *Kipping Action* (Figure 2-5)—Starting from balance point A extend your straight legs to C and back again to A. Position C represents the highest

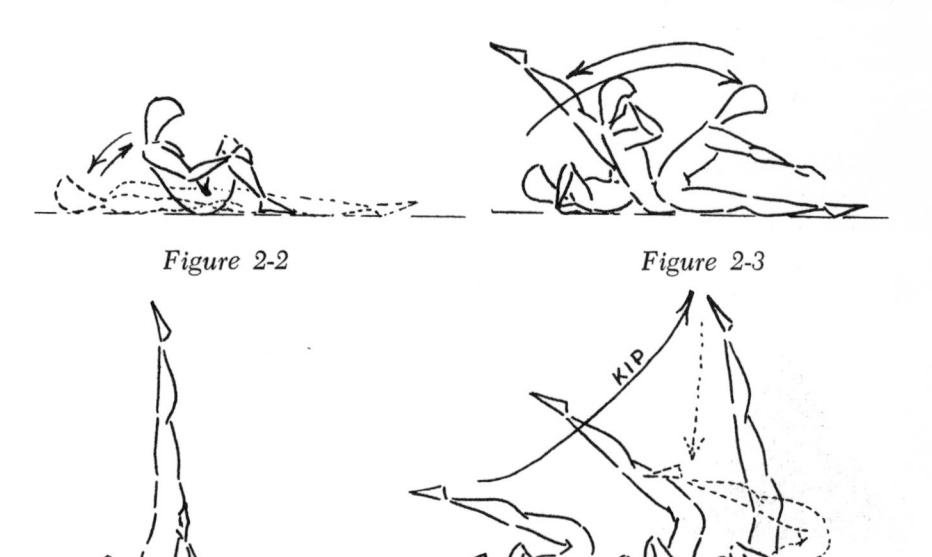

Figure 2-2　　　　　　　　　　*Figure 2-3*

Figure 2-4　　　　　　　　　　*Figure 2-5*

point you will reach without rolling forward. Extend and bend only a few degrees at first. The emphasis is on controlling a balanced position. If you roll forward as you perform adjust backward accordingly. Each extension represents a kipping action.

F. *Rolling Kip Action*—Simply combine the actions of Figures 2-3 and 2-5.

Rolling kip action will often result in backward displacement of the C. G., resulting in a crude version of a backward roll. Hence you see that kipping action can result in both forward and backward movement. Kipping action may also result in a balance position.

G. *Kip to Handstand* (Figure 2-6)—Work with a partner. We assume you can be held in a handstand position. When you extend your arms and shoot the legs straight up from a rolling kip action you will find that it is very easy to get to the handstand position with a minimum of help from a partner. Once in the handstand your partner may either help you step down or roll out.

2. APPARATUS KIPPING—The following group of movements is also in the kip family.

A. *Stem Rise on Uneven Bars* (Figure 2-7)—Just because you are a male does not automatically prevent your using the uneven parallel bars. Use of this apparatus for men can be traced back almost one hundred years although it is today a competitive event for women.

In the figure, position A shows the arms straight. The right leg is also straight and is held close to the upper bar. In B three things are happening 1. extension of the left leg with 2. thrust of the right leg on the under side of the upper bar and 3. a pull by both arms. When these

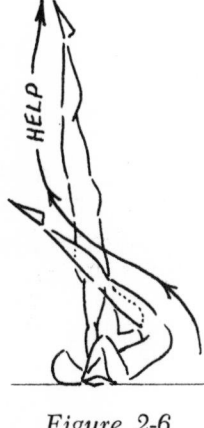

Figure 2-6

Figure 2-7

Evaluation Questions

What does the term AGILITY as used in this text include?

three actions occur simultaneously the C position (front support) is easily attained. Do you see the kipping action of the right leg? It is also important that you feel this action as you perform.

B. *Kip on the End of a Low Box* (Figure 2-8)—Observe the action of this kip. Have a partner place his hands under your hips and lift them as you kip. Your partner will stand to one side.

C. *Kips Between Two Boxes* (Figure 2-9)—The figure is viewed from above With this arrangement all three varieties of kips may be performed. The back kip and kip to handstand should be assisted, however. In the latter your partner may stand on one of the boxes. As your legs extend he will be in a position to guide your legs.

3. CASTING—Casting is another kind of gymnastic action related to swing. The cast described here is done from a front support position (Figure 2-7C); the arms are extended and help bear the weight. The cast is initiated by a short underswing of the legs opposite the direction of the

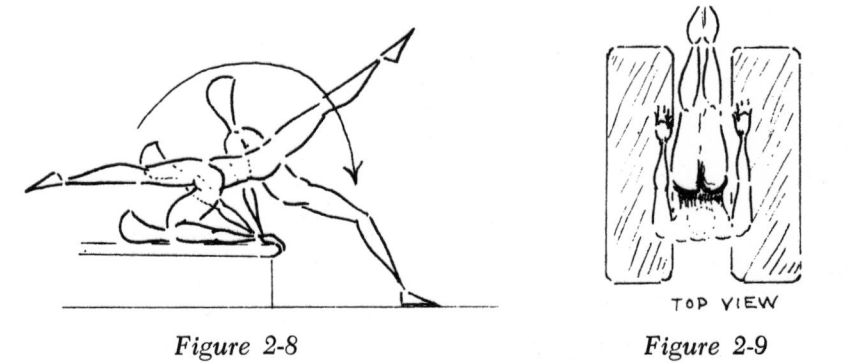

Figure 2-8   *Figure 2-9*

cast. The reaction to this initial swing results in a smooth swing of the legs in a backward direction and the shoulders move forward. Movements are then performed from ("out of") the cast. In the United States the term *cast* also refers to a particular variety of movements which are really kips performed from swing usually in a forward direction. (See Cast in the gymnastic index offered in the next chapter under parallel bars.)

    A. *Casting from the End of a Side Horse or Beam* (Figure 2-10)—In A, note the initiating leg movement. The shaded figure B has completed the forward leg swing. In C the legs are *cast* rearward. You may finish up in a variety of ways; on your knees, to your feet or simply back to sitting where you might again initiate another cast. Emphasis is placed on straight legs and arms.

    B. *Cast from a Bar* (Figure 2-11)—Note that the bar is adjusted to a low position. The cast is much the same as the one immediately above. You may finish by dropping to the mat as shown or attempt to achieve a front support. The latter takes greater control and is a good test of dynamic balance.

Figure 2-10   *Figure 2-11*

    C. *Casting from the End of a Trampoline* (Figure 2-12)—Learning to use the trampoline as a training aid is good practice for the beginner since it is so often used at the advanced level. Cast to your knees; later to your feet. If your casting action is excellent, you will find you can actually cast up to a handstand with a little help and thus prepare yourself for giant swings. (See index in next chapter under Horizontal Bar.)

    D. *Cast to Scissors on the End of the Horse* (Figure 2-13)—This is simply a variation of the cast already described. The movement out of the cast is called a scissors due to the crossing action of the legs. You finish facing away from the horse. The landing is taken on the thighs.

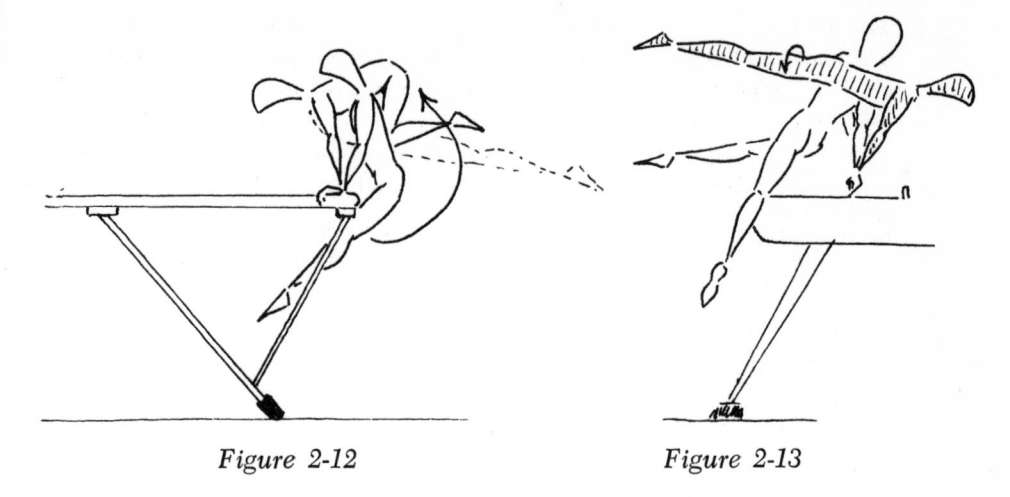

Figure 2-12   Figure 2-13

E. *Supple Movement* (Figure 2-14)—This is as close as you can come to casting on the floor. For the execution of a good supple action, the tops of the feet are on the floor rather than the typical toes curled under position of the push-up. Practice first on mats or some other soft surface. The position shown in black is high enough for a beginner.

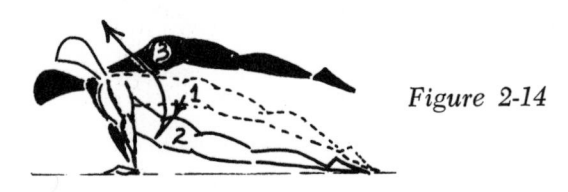

Figure 2-14

4. SWINGING (From hang)—The following movements are all true swings from a hang. Since they are relatively easy to do they should be mastered prior to swings from support which require a bit more balance and supporting strength. These actions require only the ability to hold on to apparatus with hand grips, and some abdominal strength. Once again we recommend some begining uneven bar experiences for boys and men since the apparatus permits frequent rest.

A. *Pendulum Swing*—it is virtually impossible to jump up to hang on a bar without swinging. You should experience this pendulum swing on rings and bars. By piking on the forward part of your swing you will find that you may easily increase the total arc of your back-and-forth motion.

27

B. *Generating a Swing from Hang* (Figure 2-15)—Generating a large swing from hang is a useful movement. It is learned best on a high horizontal bar. At the end of your pendulum swing (A) begin to chin yourself (B) and almost simultaneously thereafter pike at the waist, thereby accelerating the movement (C). The body is then stretched out and up so that the toes are well above the level of the bar (E), finally resulting in a fully extended position. From (F) in the diagram you will have developed sufficient swing for many subsequent movements on the bar.

C. *Generating a Swing on the Rings* (Figure 2-16)—The action is somewhat the same as for bar swinging. Since rings are not stable, you will find that swinging the body to a position parallel to the floor on both the forward and backward aspects is not an unreasonable goal. This swing is perhaps the most fundamental of all movements on the rings.

D. *Acceleration of a Swing on the Uneven Bars* (Figure 2-17)—Starting with pendulum swing (A) you are moving backward. Before reaching the ending of the backswing, quickly tuck the legs (B-C). The forward swing will be faster, and you will find no particular difficulty finishing in position (D).

E. *Underbar Pike Swing* (Figure 2-18)—From position (A) jump and pike (rotating rearward) to the rear which will result in a swing below the parallel bars in a hand support. Although the swing is shown only in a forward direction in the diagram ending in position (D), you should attempt to swing back with control. By a slight kipping action you will find that you will be able to accelerate the swing with a minimum of energy. This swing is very fundamental to intermediate and advanced work on parallel bars.

5. SWINGING (From support)—The kind of swinging you will do from support is typical of work performed above apparatus, particularly on the side horse, floor and parallel bars. If you have any difficulty performing five push-ups you will have quite a bit of trouble perfecting these movements. They should be postponed until your support strength is increased sufficiently.

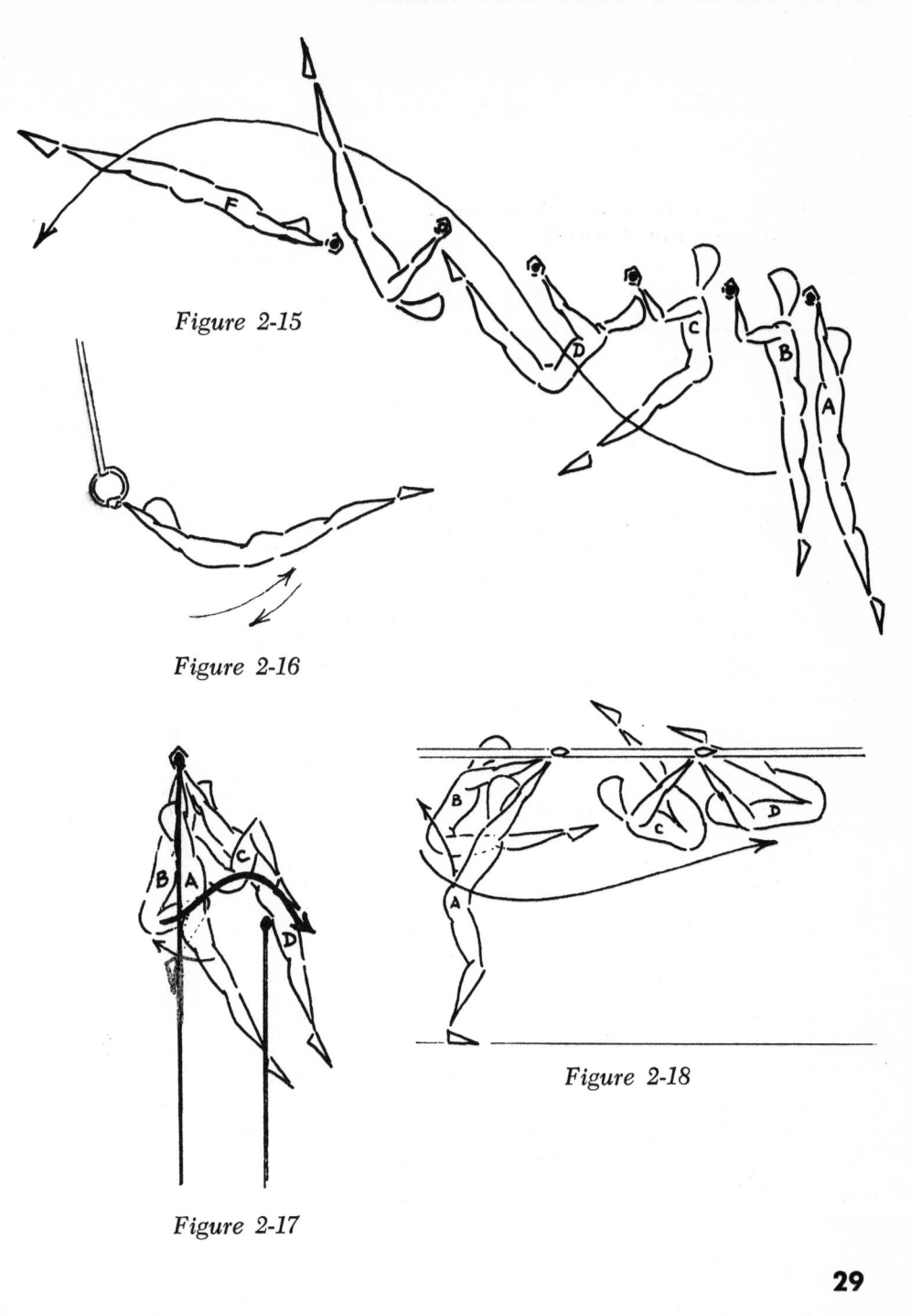

Figure 2-15

Figure 2-16

Figure 2-17

Figure 2-18

A. *Single Leg Circle* (Pinwheel) *on the Floor* (Figure 2-19)—Since this movement looks impressive to the beginner you will derive much satisfaction from the fact that it is actually quite easy to do. Once learned, you will know something of shifting your weight which is so essential in side horse performance. In the figure you observe the starting position (A). The weight is evenly distributed on the hands and the right leg (left handers may prefer the opposite arrangement). Start with a slow, determined effort to keep your swinging leg absolutely straight. At (B) the weight is momentarily transferred to the left arm. Maintain your straight leg as you lean to the left on your left arm and quickly pass the swinging leg under the bent one. Then the weight is transferred to the right arm so the swinging leg may pass easily under the left hand. With a little practice you will find the proper rhythm for weight shift. Practicing with the opposite leg is good discipline for your weak side, but one side will always feel more comfortable.

B. *Feint Swings on the Side Horse* (Figure 2-20)—From a front support (dotted) the weight is transferred to the side of the swing and the leg on that side is swung around to the feint shown on the right of the figure. Later on you will find the feint helpful in winding up for more advanced side horse movements. Practice the feint to both sides.

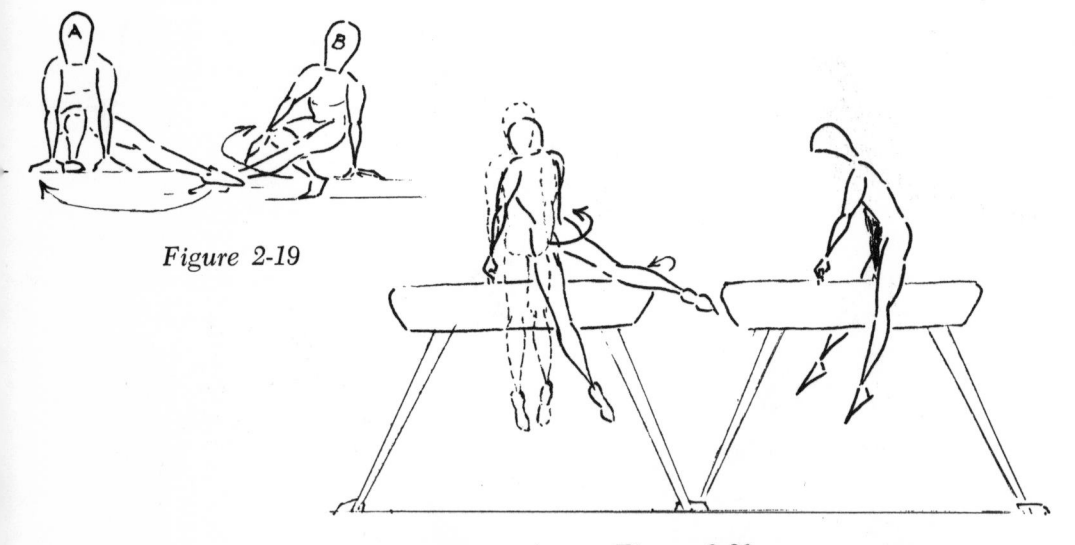

Figure 2-19

Figure 2-20

C. *Leg Cuts on the Side Horse* (Figure 2-21)—From a front support (dotted) lean the weight to one side in order to lift the leg on the opposite side which swings under the hand. (See black figure.) Once the leg is "cut" under, immediately shift the weight back to the opposite hand and swing *both* legs to the side as shown in the right portion of the figure. From here, "cut" the leg back shifting weight accordingly. When you can do the movement repeatedly to both sides, you have taken a giant step in support swinging on the side horse.

D. *Half Double Leg Circles*—These movements might better be described as vaults (flank vaults or half flank circles), but we include them here since they are done in support, and developing swing in these movements is very important.

 1. (Figure 2-22)—This is a flank vault from front support to rear support. The initiating action is shown (dotted) as a hyperextension of the body resulting in a thrust upward and to the side of the supporting arm. The legs extend away from the support arm and circle around to a position in front of the body. Getting around will be difficult until you make a dynamic effort. Check your progress by noting the number of degrees you cover. More than 180 degrees indicates you may soon shift weight and accomplish a full double leg circle. If your hand support is on a little mound of earth or sand a double leg circle is even more likely to develop with practice.

 2. *Jump to a Rear Support on the Side Horse* (Figure 2-23)—As you jump from the floor immediately transfer your weight to one arm in order that you may pass joined straight legs under the opposite hand. After practice you may try a feint to an immediate double leg circle (half) to rear support.

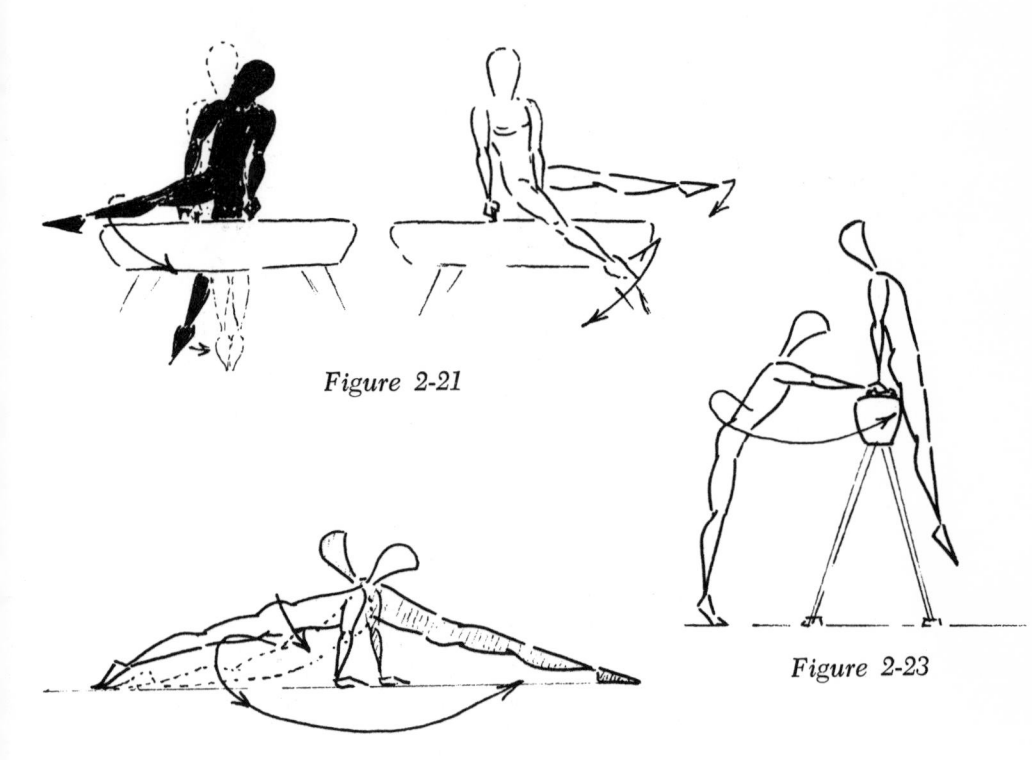

Figure 2-21

Figure 2-22

Figure 2-23

E. *Upper Arm Support Swinging* (Figure 2-24)—This first of two kinds of swing in support is performed on parallel bars. As a beginner, your approach to this swing should be gradual so your arms get used to what is often reported to be unpleasant pain under the arms. As you progress you will learn to tense these muscles and thereby avoid much (not all) of the pain. Finally you may try a run and jump into an upper arm swing as depicted in the figure.

F. *Hand Support Swinging* (Figure 2-25)—This is the second type of parallel bar swing. Work with the bars low as shown to prevent a sudden drop to the underarms. Notice the forward lean on the back swing and vice versa. Once you feel the dynamic balance of this swing you will be able to work in and out of it.

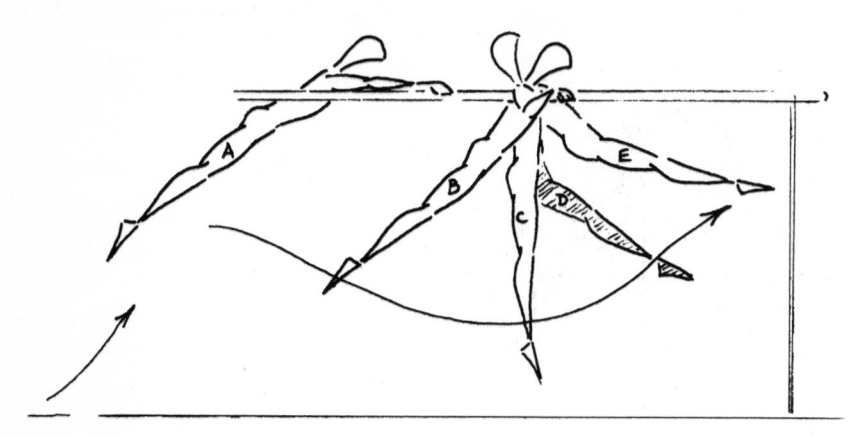

Figure 2-24

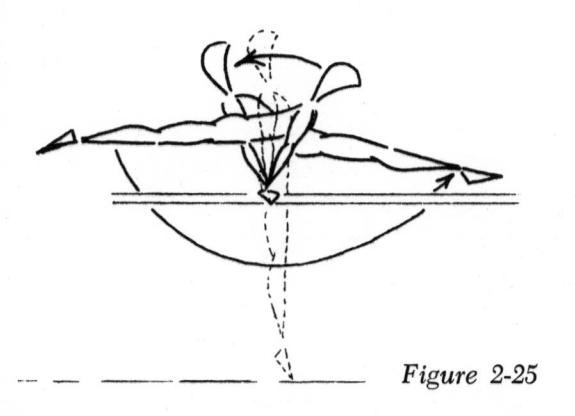

Figure 2-25

6. SHORT CIRCLE SWINGS—Short circle swings are first learned on the low horizontal bar or the uneven bars. The principle of conservation of angular momentum operates in these swings.

A. *Single Knee Swing Up* (Figure 2-26)—Hanging in the position shown by the white figure, attempt to swing gently to get the feel of the movement. After several light swings, reach upward with the free leg and pull toward the bar as the leg sweeps down. Notice how the body shortens.

B. *Kickover* (Figure 2-27)—In addition to a good swing with your preferred leg, you must be able to keep your arms bent throughout to reach (E). From (A), step under the bar with the nonswinging foot. From (B) to (C) kick the preferred leg up and back. Bending the leg slightly (dotted) will accelerate your first attempts. Try this movement from the low bar to the high bar of the unevens. Most important is that the arm pull and swinging leg work together, not in sequence.

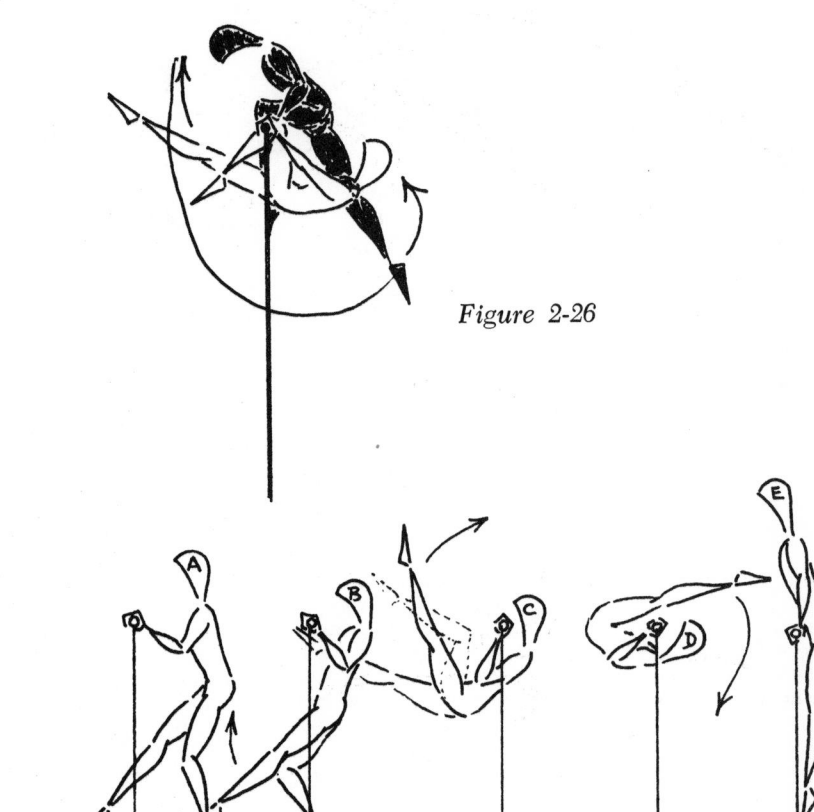

Figure 2-26

Figure 2-27

C. *Back Hip Circle* (Figure 2-28)—From a short cast from (A) to (B), the body is swung into the bar and you literally wrap yourself around the bar bending slightly at the waist. In (E) the gymnast has slowed his circle by extending the body.

D. *Front Hip Circle* (Figure 2-29)—If you are successful in performing a front hip circle, you will have experienced the "truth" of all gymnastic circles. The movement is not dangerous, but you must stretch and finally shorten the body quickly, and these actions must be done more emphatically than in any other circle. Just as the body begins to fall forward, the tight pike is dynamically performed. Tucking at first may result in early success. The first time you make it you will be pleasantly surprised.

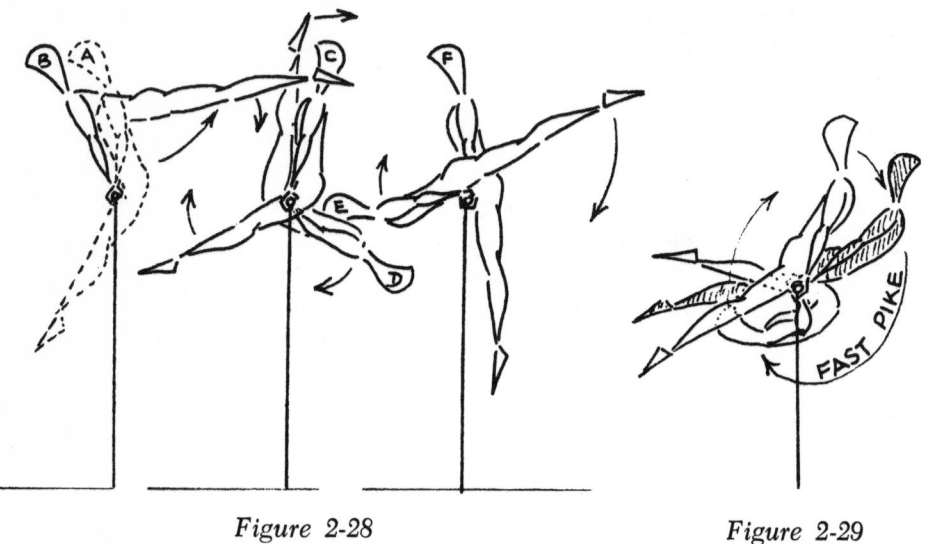

Figure 2-28   Figure 2-29

7. JUMPS AND LEAPS USING LEG SWING—The following typical jumps and leaps get their impetus from leg swing.

A. *Tour Jete* (Figure 2-30)—Swing for this turning jump is provided by the preferred (usually dominant) leg. You may land on the foot of the swinging leg (as shown) or land on the take-off foot which is a bit more difficult to control. You will find that the legs go through a scissors action during the movement. Start low and increase height and power only when you are sure of a controlled landing.

B. *Hitch Kick* (Figure 2-31)—This kind of kicking action will be familiar to the soccer player. The action of a high kicking leg is quickly balanced by a similar high kick of the other leg (scissors action). The landing is taken on the foot of the leg kicking first. Once again, increase power and height as control improves.

We thus come to the end of your initial experiences with swing. Remember that they are *not* isolated from the other elements of the "Big

Figure 2-30

Figure 2-31

Five" but usually occur in combination. The swing elements described simply depend more on swing than on the other four elements.

BALANCE

Look at each of the figures presented thus far in this chapter and apply the balance principles discussed in Chapter 1.

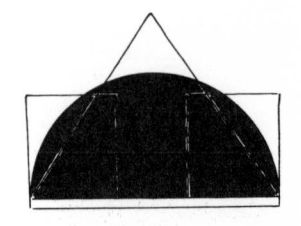

Balancing on the feet and other parts of the body is a hallmark of gymnastics. Balancing practice begins on the floor. We have also included balance beam tasks here. The beam is equally valuable for both sexes and especially so for beginners. Walking and running on a four-inch beam helps one cultivate and feel the balance common in floor work.

Have someone judge your running form using the checklist on page 39. On which items do you need practice? If all six points check out positively you should be able to vault fairly well.

Evaluation Questions

You have already been introduced to the dynamic balance necessary in apparatus work. The concentration below, therefore, is on static balance.

1. FOOT BALANCES—Static balancing on one or two feet is common and expected in floor exercise. There are lunges (fencers stance), scales and an endless variety of other positions. The candle is just one example. You will learn many others.

A. *Scales*—In Figure 2-32 you observe the front scale. The dotted figure shows the correct starting position. Rather than bending over, there is an attempt to stretch the nonsupporting leg rearupward while keeping the chest high. The side scale is shown in Figure 2-33. Once again a slow, controlled stretch into position is the desired action.

B. *Bending the Back* (Figure 2-34)—From a stand, slowly bend backward as shown. As this action takes place the hips are displaced forward to accomodate the C. G. The balanced position you finally obtain is very similar to the landing preferred in handsprings, kips and headsprings in a forward direction.

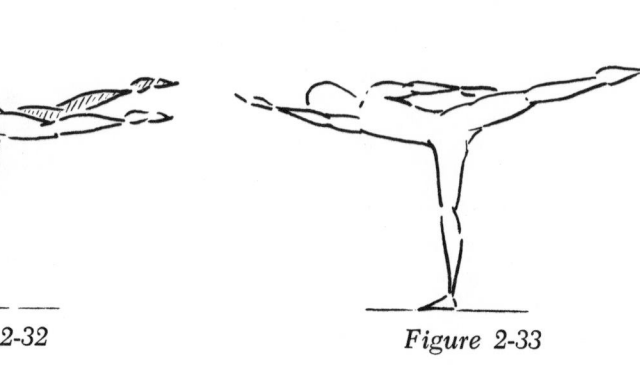

Figure 2-32   Figure 2-33

C. *Sitting Action* (Figure 2-35)—The objective here is to note the exact point in time when you fall out of balance. This training is an important prerequisite for learning a back handspring.

2. OTHER BALANCES ON THE FLOOR—We have already referred to "the balance point" (Figure 2-5). Other balances are performed on the knees and hands. Four balances have been selected for this section.

A. *Egg and V Sits* (Figure 2-36)—Having performed the balance on the hips (Egg) unfold the tucked legs to the V position. In this latter position you will feel your abdominal muscles hard at work.

B. *Head and Hand Balance* (Figure 2-37)—Commonly called headstand, first attempts should be limited to the tucked stance (knees on upper arms) shown. Beginners often try to kick up to this balance and fail. Control in an extended position will come as a result of carefully and slowly feeling your own way up. In the extended position there is no apparent bend (arch) in the back.

C. *Candle* (Figure 2-4)—See description under Swing.

D. *Balance Point* (Figure 2-5)—See section under Swing.

Note: The last two balances are repeated here to emphasize their importance. By now you should be able to combine a variety of movements with these positions.

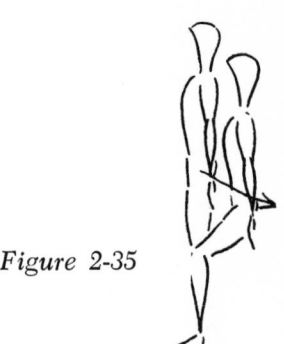

Figure 2-34

Figure 2-35

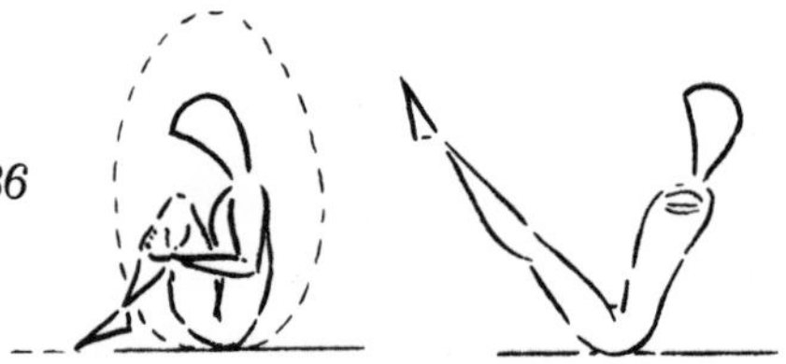

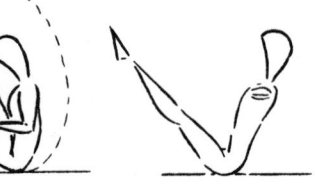

Figure 2-36

Figure 2-37

3. HAND BALANCING—The handstand has become a symbol for gymnastics. In Figure 2-38 you observe the single leg swing-up (float up) to a hand-supported position. As a beginner, do not expect to *hold* a handstand. It will come with practice. It is more important that you learn the feel of a handstand by floating up as shown. If you use a partner it will only be necessary for him to prevent your swinging leg from swinging too far. At this stage keep the nonswinging leg bent. Swing up with control and gradually attempt to stay on the hands as long as possible without falling over. With adequate practice you will finally "get stuck." This is the day you float up and stay there! One final hint, distribute the weight on your hands through the balls of the fingers and heel of each hand. The center of your hand makes no contact with the floor.

4. BALANCING ON APPARATUS—The following balances are static positions on the apparatus. Once again, the beam is used. In addition to locomotor movements on the beam in all directions, every beginner should attempt to lie down on the beam and regain the feet in a variety of ways.

A. *Dish Rag and Abdominal Balance on the Beam* (Figure 2-39)—From the dish rag (draped relaxed and balanced on the beam) raise your head and legs to an abdominal balance. With some minor adjustments you will come to know just about where you C. G. is located. Try the same experiment on the horizontal bar. Apparatus is adjusted so it is fairly close to the floor as shown.

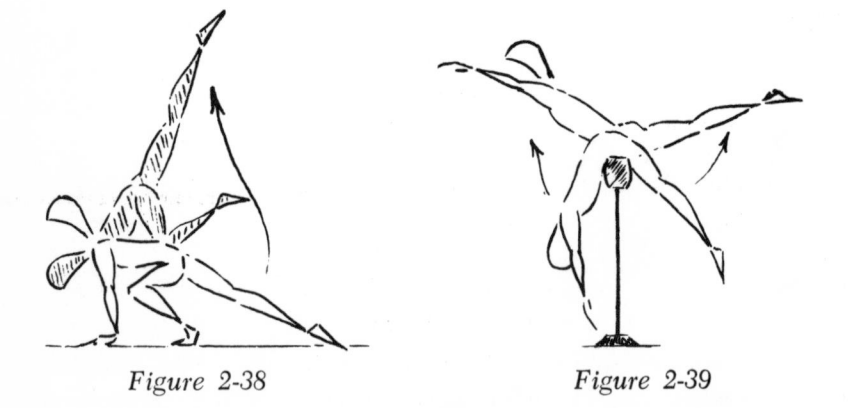

Figure 2-38   Figure 2-39

B. *Inverted Hang* (Figure 2-40)—Although first attempts are often shaky, you will master the balance for this hang in no time. Try your inverted hang on the parallel bars as well as the rings. Keep your head up! It is very difficult to control the hang when your head is centered between your arms.

C. *Upper Arm Balance Support* (Figure 2-41)—Swing up with support taken by the upper arms (Figure 2-24) or you may roll back from a straddled

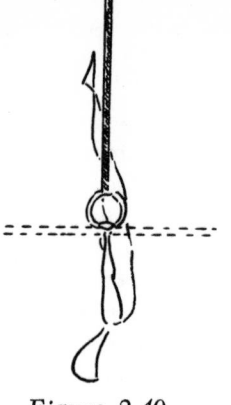

Figure 2-41

Figure 2-40

position above the bars. The hips (C. G.) are the key to maintaining balance and must be held over the supporting base.

The foregoing balances may be practiced in any order. They represent important keys to rapid advancement as an intermediate since most of these positions appear in gymnastic routines.

AGILITY

In addition to initial experiences in traditional vaulting we also include movement fundamentals such as running and tumbling in this section.

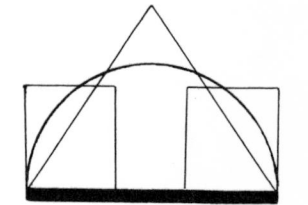

In Chair Gymnastics we have included some important agility ideas. In our swing section you were introduced to the kip but it is no less important here. Forward handsprings and headsprings are true kips but are ordinarily classified as tumbling items. The following experiences all lead to excellence in agility.

1. RUNNING—Paraphrasing Bantz we might say, "who can run, can vault and tumble." In the author's experience, natural runners have had the edge in both these activities. Are you a naturally good runner? Look at the sequence in Figure 2-42 (A-F) and consult a track specialist if you have particular difficulties. Good runners exhibit the following qualities:

A. They run relaxed.
B. They have no unnecessary side to side or twisting action.
C. Their feet are generally in line with the direction of the run.

39

D. Their arm swing is generally in line with or parallel to the direction of the run. The arms do *not* swing across the midline of the body.

E. Their arms and shoulder move together well; they do not look stiff.

F. Their heads are held naturally throughout the run.

2. THE SKIP STEP—The skip step (more properly a hop followed by a step) is probably the most common movement in tumbling. It is used to convert a run into handsprings, cartwheels and other combinations. In Figure 2-42 a run is converted to a skip step in sequence (G) to (I). The gymnast hops on the right foot and steps left. This is the way most right-handed people prefer. Right-handed (and footed) people depend on their left foot for support. The right leg is thus freed for kicking actions. If you are right handed and left footed or vice versa you will encounter a bit of

Figure 2-42

Figure 2-43

trouble in tumbling. Even though it will not seem natural at first, try to cultivate *one* strong side as a beginner. In other words try to perform either as a left hander or a right hander but not a mixture.

Once your skip step is well controlled you should attempt to move out of it. Try another skip step or a forward roll for example. Later you will learn to perform a cartwheel out of it.

3. THE HURDLE STEP (Figure 2-43 F^1–J^1)—This movement is also done from a run or a few quick steps. The sequence shown is right-side oriented. The (F^1) position is generally the same as (F) above except that the arms are held to the rear in preparation for the movement this time. If it seems inconsistent that the left foot is emphasized, remember that the left foot *is* the normal right hander's take-off foot. The hop on the right foot in skip stepping prepares the tumbler to use his left foot for the same reason, a take-off! The hurdle step is commonly used in those actions requiring what we call a "two foot take-off." Once again, plan some movement "out of" a hurdle step once it is learned.

4. THE CARTWHEEL. (Figure 2-44)—The cartwheel is a unique, gymnastic movement since it is the only one which occurs in a purely side or "wall" plane. The aerial cartwheel and side somersault are close relatives. To do a cartwheel as shown is difficult for the beginner since it is done in an erect manner in a straight line. You will learn to do one by bending your body slightly at first. Once you learn the coordination and have perfected a momentary handstand, your cartwheel will approach the one in the figure.

Right handers normally move to their left side. If you are right handed and left footed, you will have to work especially hard on this one. If you do not force yourself to be one sided, you will have difficulty combining

Figure 2-44

the cartwheel with a skip step and confound your work even more when the round-off is attempted. A round-off is a method for converting forward tumbling into backward tumbling. Essentially, the round-off *is* similar to a cartwheel with a one-fourth turn and is one of the most important keys to intermediate tumbling success.

If your cartwheel is sloppy at first, take heart in the knowledge that at your level the coordination involved, not good form, is the primary goal. Very slowly transfer your weight, hand—hand—foot—foot. Keep close to the ground until you move smoothly without noise. Then try for more elevation.

5. JUMPING DOWN FROM HEIGHTS (Figure 2-45)—Jumping down from things (Chair Gymnastics) prepares you for the kind of landing you experience in traditional vaulting. Controlled landing is the objective. When you land in control, by slight flexion at the knees, ankles and hips, you "stick" to the landing surface and do not make loud, sharp sounds. Upon landing you should generally be in balance and you should learn how to use your arms to control the balance of landing. Since arms have weight, your C. G. can be manipulated slightly by moving them forward or to the rear as needed.

Jump down in a variety of ways (make up your own) always judging your performance in terms of landing control. Then try the whole action depicted in Figure 2-45. Squat up; hop to the other side and jump down.

Figure 2-45

Height of the jump will be determined once again by landing control. The first part of this action we call a "mount." Try mounting to the surface of a beam or trampoline. Finally perform the whole action from a run. This is your basic preparation for traditional vaulting.

6. THE SQUAT VAULT (Figure 2-46)—The squat vault may be learned soon after you have mastered the work suggested immediately above. From an appropriate run, your initial thrust comes from the legs; a final thrust from the hands (B) to (C) should enable you to be well above the vault apparatus, giving you time to prepare for your landing. No springing device (springboard, trampolette, etc.) is used at this time. You must learn to use the natural spring of your legs and this is best learned without a springing device. The spring device used in advanced gymnastics is relatively stiff and is used effectively by those who learn their fundamentals. An extremely springy device can become a crutch and promotes poor control when used by beginners.

Figure 2-46

At position (A) the gymnast has just completed his hurdle step. With more experience your take-off at (A) can gradually move away from the horse. Hand placement (grips) and push-off are accomplished in (B) and (C). In (D) and (E) notice that the shoulders are ahead of the feet. If your feet lead the vault at this point, thrust has been insufficient or absent. You might practice this vault to the surface of a trampoline and attempt to land on your knees as far inboard on the bed as possible.

7. SOMERSAULTING—The somersault is an advanced movement but variations and lead-up movements are all part of the beginners work. The backward and forward rolls (tucked) on the mats are part of this preparation. Backward rolling has already been covered in part.

In the forward roll (Figure 2-47) your preparation for somersaulting progresses even farther since it is related to the somersault forward. Furthermore, as a beginner you might very well accomplish a forward somesault after a few months' work but not a back somersault. The back somersault will eventually be easier for you to do, but it requires much more groundwork in tumbling. The back somersault is best left alone until the back handspring is mastered. This work and preparation goes beyond the scope of this book.

Figure 2-47

Your immediate objective is a smooth forward roll on mats. Almost anyone can turn over in what we call a monkey roll. We expect more than that. When starting, shown in black, imagine that some device is supporting your hips as you roll. Keep your legs relatively straight until you touch the the nape of your neck. At this point, a gentle tuck will accelerate you enough so you can stand with control. Tucking too quickly and too soon causes too much speed. At first you might simply remain piked and roll forward to a sitting \position. Your arms should not collapse suddenly during a roll but slowly flex, providing a slow descent for your upper back.

With more experience, run and with a two foot take-off attempt to roll to the bed of a trampoline. You will need a partner whose job it is to touch your hips as you turn over. You will soon discover that you can turn over to your back without touching the padded end of the trampoline. Once you have done so, you will have performed a crude variation of a front somersault. If a foam rubber pit is available, you may practice the front somersault there. You may be surprised to find that even as a beginner you can "stand it up" (land in a standing position).

Having completed all of the work thus far in this chapter you will have touched on all the essentials of the gymnastic model (Figure 2-1) and especially those most central aspects. Remaining are a few suggestions about the outriggers: strength and flexibility.

STRENGTH

Remember that we have separated the "Big Five" as a matter of convenience. In most movements the five elements are combined. In terms of strength you have already experienced:

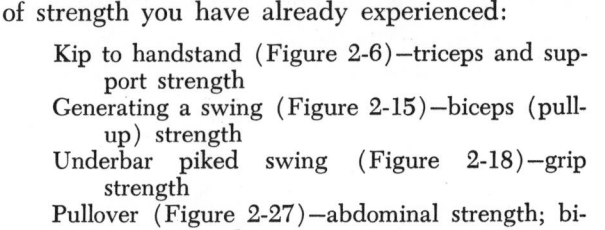

Kip to handstand (Figure 2-6)—triceps and support strength

Generating a swing (Figure 2-15)—biceps (pull-up) strength

Underbar piked swing (Figure 2-18)—grip strength

Pullover (Figure 2-27)—abdominal strength; biceps strength

"V" Sit (Figure 2-36)—abdominal strength

Additional strength suggestions have been provided in Chapter 1. These exercises and suggestions are sufficient for the beginner, but we would like to add just two more strength items in this section, the muscle up on the rings and a Swedish fall.

Sometimes called the pull-push, this movement is a fundamental for strength work on the rings. It will probably be the first way you learn to gain support on the rings. In order to perform the "muscle up" properly, you need to know how to take a "false" grip. As you hang from the rings, normally you do not have a "false" grip. The normal grip is shown at the left of Figure 2-48. To obtain a "false" grip, have someone support

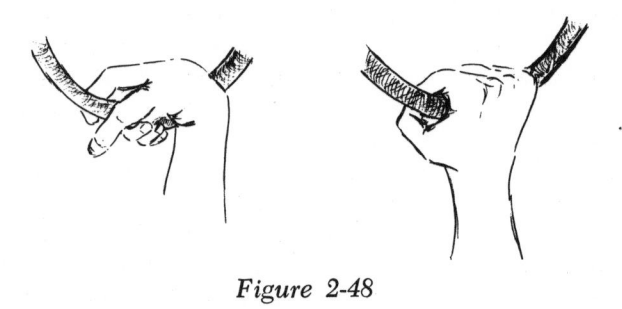

Figure 2-48

your hips as you hang, then simply rotate your hands over the rings pulling your hands together so that the heels of the hands are in contact with the rings as shown. Now chin yourself; turn your hands out and you will find that you are in a low dip position. At this point a vigorous push (with help at first) will result in a support above the rings. Once in support you may be a bit shaky at first, but very quickly you will learn to control the shakes and even perform an "L" by raising your straight legs so they are parallel with the floor. (An "L" is shown in the Chair Gymnastics sequence.)

A Swedish fall is also in the support-strength category. From a stand or scale you fall forward and take the weight gently on the hands, finishing as in Figure 2-49. The arms must learn to take up the shock of landing much as the legs are trained in vault landings.

Figure 2-49

FLEXIBILITY

You have already experienced the role of flexibility in the following:

Kipping action (Figure 2-5)—hamstring stretch and wrist flexibility

Supple movement (Figure 2-14)—suppleness in the back and ankles

Underbar piked swing (Figure 2-18)—again hamstring stretch

Hitch kick and tours jêté (Figures 2-30 & 2-31) —splits action

Scale (Figure 2-32)—splits action

Scale (Figure 2-33)—side splits action

Back bending (Figure 2-34)—back flexibility

If you are naturally stiff you will be restricted in performing any of the above movements. Training for flexibility improvement needs to be practiced daily as suggested in Chapter 1.

Our final suggestion on flexibility is to practice a skin the cat swing on the horizontal bar (Figure 2-50). You may not have immediate success with this swing since it does tax the hamstrings and requires loose shoulders.

When performed correctly, the gymnast moves from (A) to (E) and back again to (A) and does so in such a way that the movement is smooth and can be immediately repeated. It is actually a preparation for some of the advanced giant swings, but for beginners it provides an interesting flexibility challenge. It is also an excellent problem in dynamic balance. Tuck your legs through at first, but remember that tucking accelerates movement and you will quickly need to stretch out again to continue moving properly.

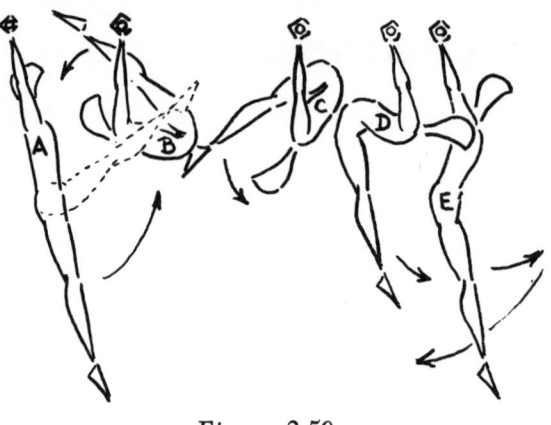

Figure 2-50

Your initial experience with gymnastics is thus complete. If you and a partner are able to share in all this work, you will be at the doorstep of intermediate gymnastics. The intermediate needs the careful guidance of an experienced, gymnastic specialist. Although most of the work above can be accomplished in the absence of such a person, the pitfalls from this point on are many and complicated. For this reason we have included a checklist in Chapter 4 which is designed to give you special help in analyzing intermediate and advanced work you are apt to encounter in other gymnastic volumes. This guide for outside reading is especially recommended when you cannot locate a specialist.

The Language of Gymnastics and an Index to Advanced Skill

The language of gymnastics is complicated and very confusing. Although some countries have worked out a fairly consistent nomenclature, such is not the case in the United States.

Our terminology is derived in a number of ways:

1. From the French, German and Spanish languages (*Kip*, Gr.; *Somersault*, Sp.; *Arabesque*, Fr.)
2. From the names of gymnasts who have popularized certain movements (*Moore*, early U.S. gymnastic leader; *Takemoto*, coach of Japanese Olympians; *Stalder*, famous Swiss gymnast)
3. From the actual sound made by the action of the movement (*Flic-flac* or *flip-flop* in one variation or another used throughout the world. Said rapidly and repeatedly, you have some idea of the sound of a back handspring.)
4. From formal gymnastic nomenclature (*Side stand, cross stand, flank*, etc., are examples of the early translations of formal German nomenclature.)

   Note: More of this terminology "in a nutshell" is found in *Women's Gymnastics*.[4]

You have already been exposed to a wide selection of gymnastic terminology in this book. As you use the language more it will take on meaning. Perhaps you will even contribute to it someday.

The remainder of this chapter is devoted to a special kind of index. It will further acquaint you with the language of gymnastics. The sequences presented are complete routines of former gymnastic champions. Each of the six international events constituting the gymnastic all-around are pre-

---

[4]Frederick, A. Bruce, *Women's Gymnastics*, Dubuque, Iowa: Wm. C. Brown Company Publishers, 1966, pp. 51-56. (Material applies to both men and women.)

sented. Many of the movements listed in the index have already been introduced. For example, you will find a forward roll variation under floor exercise.

You are *not* expected to learn these movements. The author selected the routines and vaults to display advanced work in routine constructions. They are typical rather than in the class of the most difficult. The purpose here is to acquaint you with the best so you may speak intelligently about gymnastics and appreciate more those occasional programs you view on film or television.

The routine will also become your goal. Eventually you should be able to perform routines in every gymnastic event. As a beginner, it is not your goal to create a routine. You must learn the vocabulary and construction of a foreign language before you speak or write in it with fluency.

As you approach the intermediate level you will concentrate on routines designed *for* you, not *by* you. Gymnastic specialists throughout the world are expected to compose suitable work for novices, which includes a wide diversity of fundamentals. Two very good sources are available from American publishers.[5]

AN INDEX TO ADVANCED GYMNASTICS

FLOOR EXERCISE (Boris Shaklin, Russia, All-Around Olympic Champion) Refer
to floor exercise sequence.
Arched Jump (Hollow Jump)—18.
Back Handspring—1-3 Step out 1/2 turn left (L); 13-14; 69-70.
Back Somersault—15-17; 71-73 Layout back somersault.
Cartwheel—62-64.
Double Leg Circle—48-49 This movement is extremely difficult to perform
on the floor.
Forward Handspring—21-24 Handspring done to a single leg, right (R).
Forward Roll—30-33 From a handstand; 37-42 Diving forward roll; 42-46
Pike (straight leg) forward roll; 54-55 Roll forward to kip position.
Front Somersault—7-11 Front somersault with a step out.
Handstand—25-26 Kick to handstand with one straight leg; 28-30 Tuck
jump to handstand; 52-54 Push to handstand from knees.
Handstand (Cont.) 26-28 Snap down from handstand (Mule kick).
Jumps—17-19 Arched jump; 3-4 Tour jêté.
Kick—20 High kick in preparation for tumbling sequence.
Kips—55-58 Kip, full turn to rear support ("Healy").
Round-Off (Arabian Jump)—11-13; 66-69 To place gymnast in position for
back tumbling.

[5]William Vincent, *Let's Teach Routines*, Santa Monica, Cal.: Sundby Publications, 1968 (P. O. Box 611).
James Farkas, *Age Group Workbook*, Tucson, Arizona: The United States Gymnastic Federation, 1964 (P. O. Box 4699).

Scale—47 Shows position immediately preceding scale.

Supports (Front)—51; 50-51 Rear support to front support; 59; 58-59 Rear support to front support.

Supports (Rear)—50; 58.

Turns—33-36 One- and one-half turns L.; 60-62 Counterswinging the arms with a 1/2 turn L.; 3-4 Tour jêté.

VAULTING (Takashi Ono, Former Olympic Silver Medalist in Vaulting performing a handspring and Yukio Endo, Former Olympic All-Around Champion performing a hecht; Both men have been members of the Japanese Olympic Team) Refer to the vaulting sequences.

Hurdle Step—6-7; 16-18 Notice that both steps are relatively close to the floor (skimming action).

Landing—13-15; 23-25 Both landings were held, meaning that the gymnasts needed no small steps to correct balance.

Layout—12; 22 Both gymnasts show full extension of the body prior to landing, which is a requirement.

Post Flight—11-15; 22-25.

Pre Flight—8-10; 19-21.

Push-Off—10-11; 21-22.

Run—1-5.

Take-Off—7-8; 18-19 Note the angle of take-off is more upward than forward.

PARALLEL BARS (Miroslav Cerar, Yugoslavia, Former All-Around European Champion and Gold Medalist on Side Horse in 1964 Olympics) Refer to parallel bar sequence.

Back Somersault Catch (Performed from support to support)—38-44 Note the extreme bend of the bar in 40.

Cast (Actually swinging kips with release and regrasp)—5-11 Cast, 1/2 turn to upper arm support; "Finnish Kip" 50-53.

Front Somersault Dismount (Front-Off)—67-71 Front-off with 1/2 turn.

Front Uprise—11-14; 65-67.

Front Vault Mount—1-4 Front vault mount through planche.

Glide—25-26 In preparation for a glide kip overbar.

Glide Kip—25-31 Glide kip (overbar) to "L".

Handstand—30-36 From L pull with straight legs and arms (with legs passing through the arms) to a handstand; 57-60 Straight body press to a handstand.

Moore—15-18 High Moore (Actually a swinging back pirouette) Pirouette is the name given to turns on the parallel bars while in handstand position.

Pirouette—15-18 Back swinging (no held position) pirouette; 35-38 1/2 pirouette to a regular handstand.

Planche—If held, the positions shown in 20 or 39 would be true planches.

Rear Uprise—53-55 (Note "Banana Back" at position 54.)

Rear Vault—20-26 Rear vault to glide.

Straddle Catch (Double Cut Catch)—From rear uprise straddle catch to "L".

Stutz (Stützekehre)—44-49 Note at point 48 that there is a complete release of both hands; 61-65 to upper arms.

Support Swing—13-15 Take note of the shift of weight.

Under Bar Swing—50-51.

Upper Arm Swing—10-12.

HORIZONTAL BAR (Performed by Takashi Ono, Former Olympic Gold Medalist
on the horizontal bar)

Back Kip—19-22 The rear of the body leads the movement.

Free Hip Circle—28-30 Free hip circle to handstand.

Full Pirouette (Full Turn)—40-46 This movement is actually one full turn
during the execution of a front giant swing.

Full Turn Catch—13-18 The turn is made from a release on the back swing to a regrasp.

German Giant Swing—22-26 Actually an undislocated giant swing; 26-28 1/2 turn to a regular (over) grip from a "German" giant.

Giant Swing—Back Giant Swings 5-7; 30-32. Front Giant Swings 37-39; 53-56.

Grip Changes (Commonly called simply "changes")—7-8 Overgrip to undergrip; From 39-40 the left hand is changed from an overgrip to an undergrip; 51-53 from overgrip to undergrip.

Hecht—56-61 Hecht dismount from front giant swing (Note "Banana Back").

Kip—19-22 This is a back kip, at position 22 the gymnast has not quite achieved support but did cast into the "German" giant swing immediately after this frame. 49-51 Regular kip.

Rear Vault—45-49 This is another release and regrasp movement performed out of a front giant swing.

Stalder Circles (Stalder Shoot)—33-36 Back Stalder circle.

Stoop Through (Jam)—8-12 Stoop through in this instance is immediately followed by a full turn which in turn is followed by a full turn catch. The sequence in its entirely is a form of a movement sequence called a Takemoto.

Underswing—1-4 Underswing 1/2 turn.

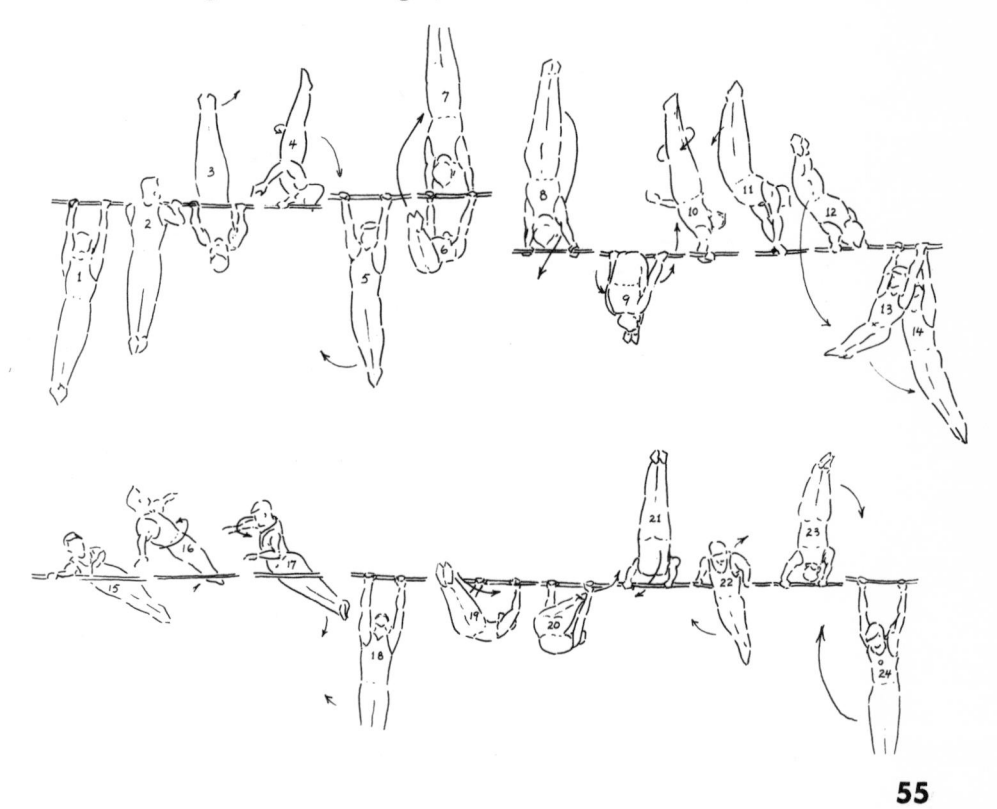

RINGS (Performed by Yuri Titov of Russia, former World All-Around Champion and Gold Medalist on Rings at the World Games in Prague in 1962.) Refer to ring sequence.

Back Lever—40.

Cross (Crucifix)—15-18 Lower straight arms to "L" cross; 26-29 Lower straight body to regular cross.

Dislocate—3-6; 32-34; 45-47.

Flex (Piked Inverted Hang)—1-3 Pull to flex; 30-32 Pull straight body to flex.

Front Lever—38-44 Back roll through back lever (40) to front lever.

Front Support (or more simply "support")—37; 25 "L" support.

Giant Swing—10-15 Front Giant swing (From handstand to handstand).

Handstand—10; 15; 26; 25-26 Press to handstand.

Hang—1 Regular hang; 41 Dislocate hang.

Inlocate—19-23 Straight body inlocate.

Kip—23-25 Kip to "L" support.

"L"—25; 18 "L" cross.

Planche—If 16 were a held position it would be called a planche.

Scale to Handstand—12-15 (This sequence is really the last portion of Titov's front giant swing.)

Shoot (Streüli)—5-10 Shoot to handstand; 34-37 Shoot to momentary support.

Straddle Dismount (High Straddle-Off)—From dislocate 46-50.

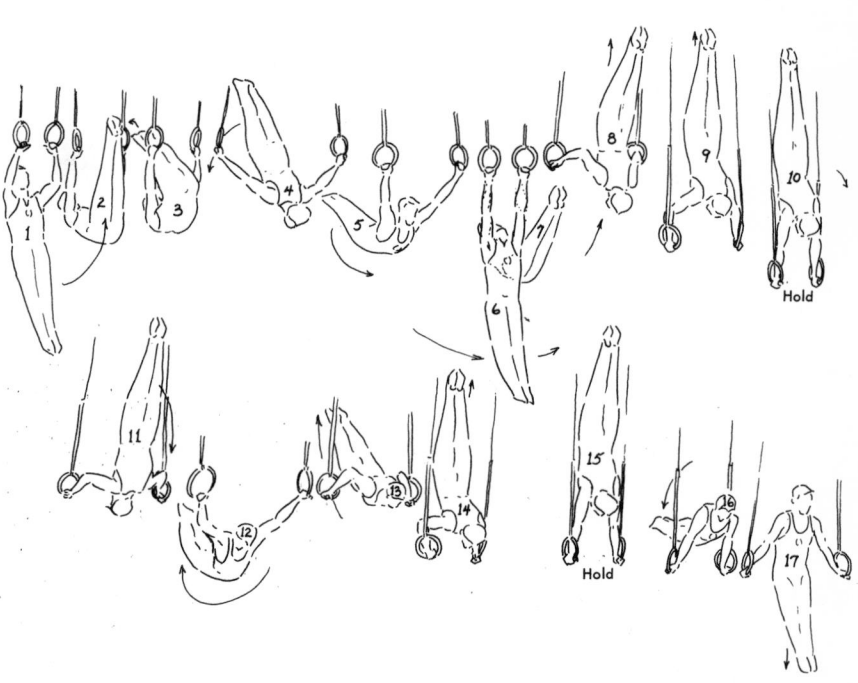

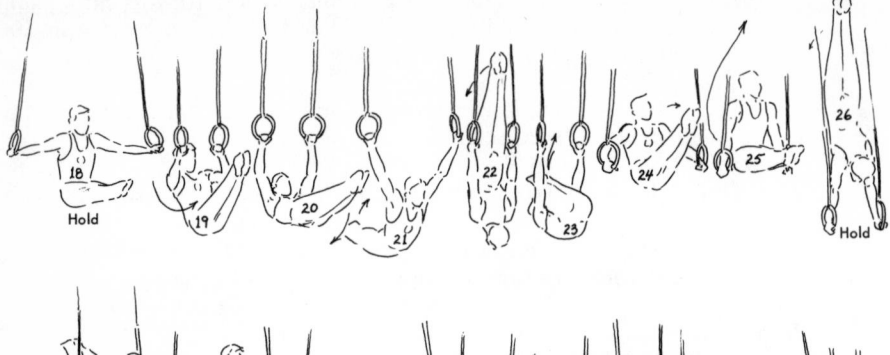

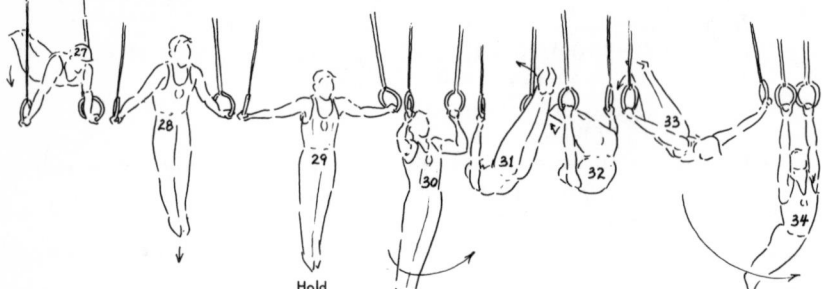

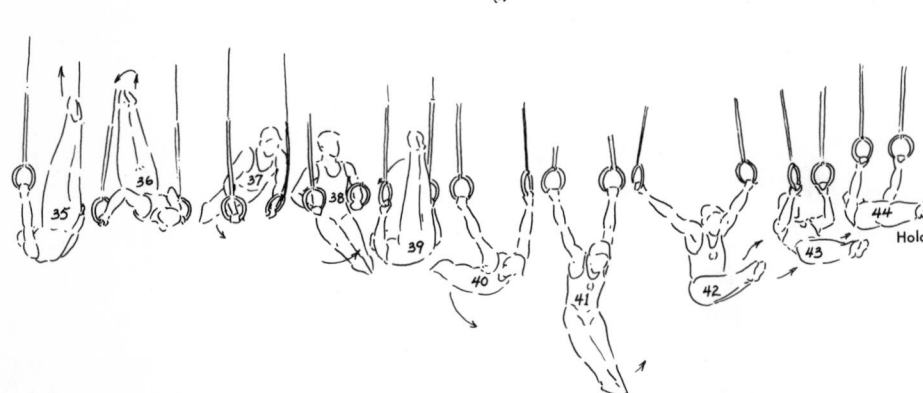

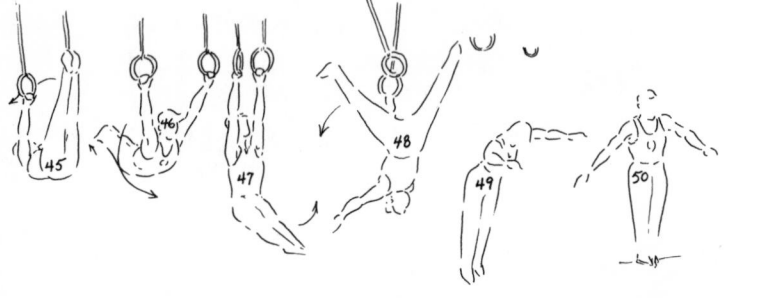

SIDE HORSE (Performed by Boris Shaklin of Russia) Refer to side horse sequence.

Double-In (Kehre)—"In" refers to the end position which is "in" the center of the horse. "Out" is used when the gymnast moves from the center to either end; 1-3 Double in mount; 35-37.

Double Leg Circles—Counterclockwise circles 3-5; 22-25; 29-31; 37-40; 48-51 without using pommel; Clockwise circle 11-12.

Double-Out (Kehre)—12-14.

Loop—44-48 Loop on end; 53-58 Loop dismount.

Moore—25-29; 49-53 Moore on the end of the side horse.

Scissors—Back scissors (swing of legs is rearward) 5-11 Two back scissors in a row; Front scissors 18-21.

Single Leg Circle—14-16 On end with 1/2 turn to center of horse.

Tromlet (Travel)—A travel or movement carrying the body from one part of the horse to another. In a tromlet the travel is executed while performing double leg circles, 31-35; 40-44.

Although the gymnasts whose work is illustrated have all excelled in one or more events, all are excellent all-around gymnasts.

Spotting: The Detective Work of Gymnastics

There are two ways to think about spotting. In the most commonly accepted sense, spotting refers to precautionary measures employed to assure the safety of a performer. The spotter takes a position best suited to the safety of his charge, ready to catch him or assist him if necessary. This is the safety domain of spotting.

Spotting may also refer to and describe certain techniques which are instructional or assistive in nature. This is the instructional domain of spotting. We therefore describe instructional spotting as the detective work of gymnastics. When your clues and cues are properly arranged, both you and your partner-assistants (P-As) can function intelligently and logically.

Fear and disorganized action of the entire organism (mind and body) are two leading stumbling blocks in gymnastics. If you are scared or lack coordination, you will probably not perform well, if at all. If you take on too much too soon your efforts can easily be frustrated.

A coordinated movement is one in which appropriate parts of your body are successfully harmonized in seemingly effortless action. Moving in a coordinated fashion varies with the learners; as in any kind of learning, some people can accomplish more than others. Time needed for learning is also a variable. If you have already gained a new appreciation of your potential by virtue of the contents thus far, you will know something about your learning style.

Let us begin with some thoughts about clues to performance.

COORDINATION

Before attempting anything new, glance through the following suggestions and checklist. Even the experienced gymnast is likely to learn by

Can you balance a handstand in the swimming pool? What other gymnastic movements can you do in the water?

Evaluation Questions

such review or at least recall to mind something important that can be, or has been, forgotten.

1. START ON THE FLOOR

A. Extract the familiar movements you perceive in something you have selected to learn or spot. You pass through a variation of a handstand while doing a cartwheel. A handspring contains kipping action.

B. Can you perform less difficult, related movements? In general they should be mastered first.

C. Does the apparatus movement under consideration have a similar "relative" that can be performed on mats? Have you mastered the floor version(s)?

2. RHYTHM—Can you identify the rhythm of a movement? Do you know its sounds? Rhythm is to music what coordination is to movement. As an example, refer to the round-off, back handspring (sequence 11-14, floor exercise, index chapter). When correctly performed, you should hear three distinct beats or sounds starting with the landing from the round-off and ending with the foot landing of the back handspring. In Figure 4-1 you see how the feet, hands, feet action might be perceived as three rhythmic beats (1, 2, 3), each having a rhythmic value in terms of time and intensity. In a good performance, the sounds have almost equal value and are equally spaced. In a poor performance, the first beat is heavy, and a pause is noticeable prior to the completion of beats 2 and 3. You may thus hear as well as see correct performance. Many performers report that they hear imagined sounds as they perform. Divers, trampolinists and dancers use this "inner music" to give them clues to timing and general performance. So can you.

Performing a movement in the imagination is a beneficial way of practicing. Mental practice actually involves specific muscles you need to use in actual performance. Therefore, before attempting new movements:

A. Watch the movement (film or live).
B. Know the sounds of the movement.
C. Invent "inner sounds" for the movement.
D. Imagine the movement.

3. PANTOMIME—A pantomimed movement is one in which an entire action or some of its parts are simulated. Pantomime helps you learn the feel of the movement.

A. Is it possible to lift (or be lifted) the performer through the movement? Emphasis is on slowness.
B. Can a stick or other object (mannequin) be used in a simulation of the movement?
C. Can it be simulated in the water? In the water one can often slow down to the point where real insight to performance can be perceived. Water also provides a generally safe environment.
D. Many movements can be safely simulated on a trampoline. The trampoline is often used as a learning device.
E. Can it be simulated on the floor? The rhythm of a cartwheel is 1, 2, 3, 4. These numerals represent hand, hand, foot, foot. To pantomime the cartwheel, simply place the hands and feet on the floor in the correct order. It might be a far cry from the cartwheel itself, but it represents just one more way to reinforce its ultimate performance.

4. PROGRESSION—Think of progression as *whole* action parts of the movement you have selected. A pie is a whole creation. So is a crust; so are blueberries. Yet the latter ingredients (wholes) are parts of the whole pie. They are related, internal wholes. A forward roll is a related, internal whole of a forward somersault. Progression to the forward somersault includes a forward roll. What are the related, internal wholes of the movement you have selected?

To design a progression, select whole, related actions. If they are related and are placed in an approximate order of difficulty, they represent a progression.

5. EXPLOSIVENESS—Explosiveness is the speed-force factor of coordination. Without it, actions diminish to sluggishness and skilled performance is impossible. What are the speed-force factors of your movement? Where and how can additional force be given to the performer? Should the run be faster? Is additional strength or flexibility needed?

A. How might the performer be turned faster?
B. Is greater running speed indicated?
C. Are the arms or legs kicking and swinging with enough speed?

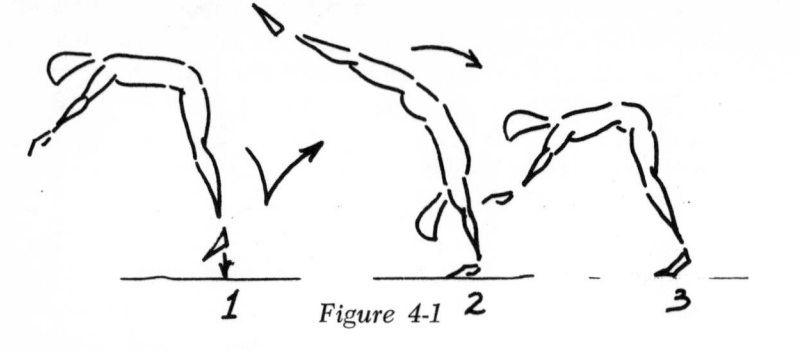

Figure 4-1

D. Is a tighter tuck, pike or stretch needed?
E. What kind of strength seems to be lacking?
F. Are you too loose?

You may simply not have the personality for quick, "nervous," dynamic action. If you are quiet, slow-moving and somewhat withdrawn in your normal relationships with people, explosiveness may be difficult for you to attain.

FEAR

Fear is the friendly enemy of the gymnast, friendly in the sense that it may very well prevent you from foolishly destroying yourself. It is an enemy of movement, however. You will not be able to perform efficiently (or at all) if it is present to any abnormal degree. To help eliminate fear we offer the following suggestions.

1. *Eliminate Height*
   A. Can the movement be performed at a lower height?
   B. If the movement is to be performed on apparatus, can its action be performed on the floor?
   C. Is it possible to set up a platform, padded if necessary, to provide for landings when first attempts to perform apparatus movements are undertaken. (See Figure 4-2.)
   D. Can your P-A get into a better position by standing on a platform, box or other apparatus? Sometimes fear is eliminated by the closeness of an assistant.
2. *Hand Spotting or Hand Assistance*
   (Review mechanical principles in Chapter 1.)
   A. Determine the critical point of the movement.
   B. The P-A should be in a position of greatest benefit to the performer without in any way hindering his action.
   C. Both you and your P-A should understand the actions of performance and assistance.
   D. The P-A's hands should be protected. He is often in a more dangerous position than the performer!

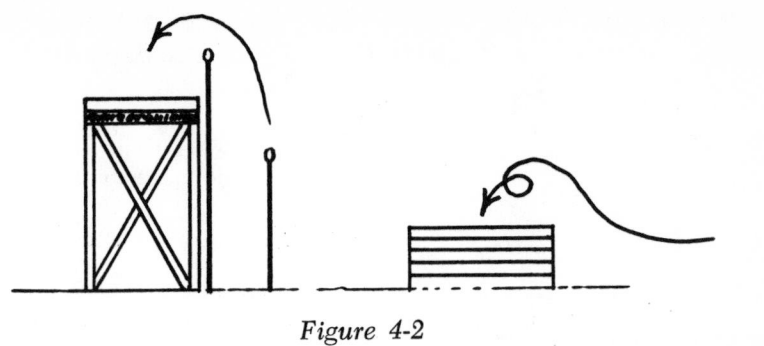

Figure 4-2

E. Practice the assisting action in other ways. Prepare yourself as a P-A by spotting actions of skilled performers. By so doing you will have the opportunity to judge your skill. If you find that you consistently misjudge your assisting action, you should *not* assist the learner who is dependent on you.

F. Verbal directions, if needed, should be short and to the point. Lengthy directions are often misunderstood.

3. *How Can Landings Be Made Softer?*
Consult the checklist for some idea starters.

4. *Belt Spotting*
Belt spotting should only be used by experienced, gymnastic specialists. In improper hands the belt can do much harm and even though some dangers are avoided, the compensation in this direction is not sufficient to warrant its indiscriminate use. Many experienced teachers avoid belts because they do not believe the proper feel of the movment is conveyed to the learner in the belt.

5. *Standard Equipment for Spotting and Partner Assistance*
A. Can dismounts or vaults be done to the surface of a trampoline?
B. Stand on apparatus to raise your level of support in partner assistance.
C. Use a ramp arrangement. Place a mat over a standard springboard. Movements (without a run) may then be performed downhill.
D. Can vaulting boxes be used?

6. *Homemade Spotting aids*
A. Beach towels may be rolled lengthwise and secured with tape.
B. Strips of cellular foam can be used creatively to prevent bruises and provide padding.
C. A canvas net can be constructed (5' x 9') to which six heavy duty, canvas handles on each long edge are attached. Sewing should be done by a shoemaker. Such nets may be used to catch performers in various ways.
D. Rolled mats and piles of the new flat-fold mats make excellent platforms and take-off substitutes.

The following checklist is a convenient summary of the suggestions given in this chapter and selected portions of Chapters 1 and 2. Skim through it when you are learning or trying to understand the specific actions of a new movement.

A CHECKLIST FOR SPOTTING AND LEARNING GYMNASTICS

I. Do you understand the movement? Can you place it on the model in Chapter 2? (Figure 2-1)
  A. What is it called; what does it look like?
    1. Are movies or loop films available?*
    2. Can you get a skilled performer to demonstrate it?
  B. Which of the "Big Five" best characterizes the movement?
    1. Is it in the swing category?
      a. In a hang?
      b. In a support?
    2. Again thinking of the swing category . . .
      a. Is it a circle with a vertical path on a bar?
      b. Is it another sort of circle on apparatus?
      c. Is it an aerial circle (somersault)?
      d. Is it a circle on the floor with a path parallel to the floor?
      e. Is it a circular floor movement with a vertical path?
        (1) Handspring? (2) Headspring? (3) Roll?
      f. A cast? (Action-reaction swing from support)
      g. A kip? On apparatus or floor?
        (1) Dead kip (2) Swinging kip
    3. Is it in the balance category?
      a. Static balance
      b. Dynamic balance? (Balance in motion)
    4. Is it in the agility category?
      a. Is it a tumbling movement?
      b. Is it one of the traditional vaults?
      c. Is it a locomotor or dance movement?
    5. Is it in the strength category?
      a. Support strength?
      b. Grip strength?
      c. Abdominal strength?
      d. Arm strength?
      e. Leg strength?
    6. Is it in the flexibility category?
      a. A split?
      b. Is backbending involved?
      c. Is there a hamstring stretch?
      d. Is it a side-bending movement?
  C. What mechanical principles are involved?
    1. Is C. G. a factor?
      a. C. G. in a bar circle? (Extend on the way down; pull in on the way up.)
      b. C. G. in a circle parallel to the ground?
      c. C. G. in balance?
      d. Can the performer be spotted or assisted near the C. G.?
    2. How are each of Newtons Laws of Motion involved?
      a. Law of inertia?
      b. Law of acceleration?
      c. Law of action-reaction (Jet propulsion)?
    3. Is a lever or moment involved? How?
    4. In what ways are the axes of the body involved?

*The Athletic Institute (805 Merchandise Mart, Chicago, Ill.) has a wide selection of gymnastic loop films.

II. How is the movement coordinated?
 A. Can the coordination be learned on the floor?
  1. Are there familiar movements contained in it?
  2. Should an easier movement be mastered first?
  3. If an apparatus movement, can a similar movement be done on the floor?
 B. What is the rhythm of the movement?
  1. What are its sounds?
  2. Can you visualize the movement?
 C. Can the movement be pantomimed?
  1. Can you be lifted through it?
  2. Can it be simulated with a stick or other object?
  3. Can it be done in water?
  4. Can it be simulated on the trampoline?
 D. Can you design a progression (program) of five to ten steps?
 E. Is there an explosive element?
III. Is the performer afraid? Why?
 A. Can height be eliminated in practice?
 B. What kind of hand assistance might you consider?
  1. What is the critical or dangerous point?
   a. Bottom of a vertical circle?
   b. Does the C. G. need to be higher?
   c. Is loss of grip possible?
   d. Are the head, neck or back in any danger?
   e. Are the assistant's hands or arms in danger?
   f. Is a jump or vault involved?
  2. What is the position of the P-A or spotter?
  3. Do you understand the action of assistance or spotting?
  4. Is the spotter in danger? How?
  5. Should some easier movements be assisted first?
  6. Are any verbal directions needed?
 C. How can the landing be made softer?
  1. Additional mats?
  2. Foam rubber scraps?
  3. Trampoline?
  4. Water?
  5. Sand or sawdust pits?
  6. Other?
 D. Should the movement be done in a belt? Is an experienced belt spotter available?
 E. Can standard equipment be used?
 F. What assistance apparatus can be made?
 G. Is there a special kind of rigging that might be employed?

USING THE CHECKLIST—THE HANDSPRING FORWARD (FIGURE 4-3)

The forward handspring belongs to that portion of gymnastics termed *agility* in this book. It is specifically a tumbling movement with a kipping action. You can visualize the kipping action by covering the top leg of (C) in the sequence and following the arrow. The trailing leg is about to kip at this point. Other areas of the "Big Five" involved in the handspring are:

1. Backbending of the dynamic variety is involved (D).
2. Splitting of the legs is noted in (B). Good splitting action makes for good handsprings. Hamstring stretch is also noticeable in (B).
These items are specifically in the domain of flexibility.
3. A strength element is identified in (C), where a vigorous push from the floor helps elevate the gymnast.
4. The swing of the straight legs can be imagined in (B) and (C).

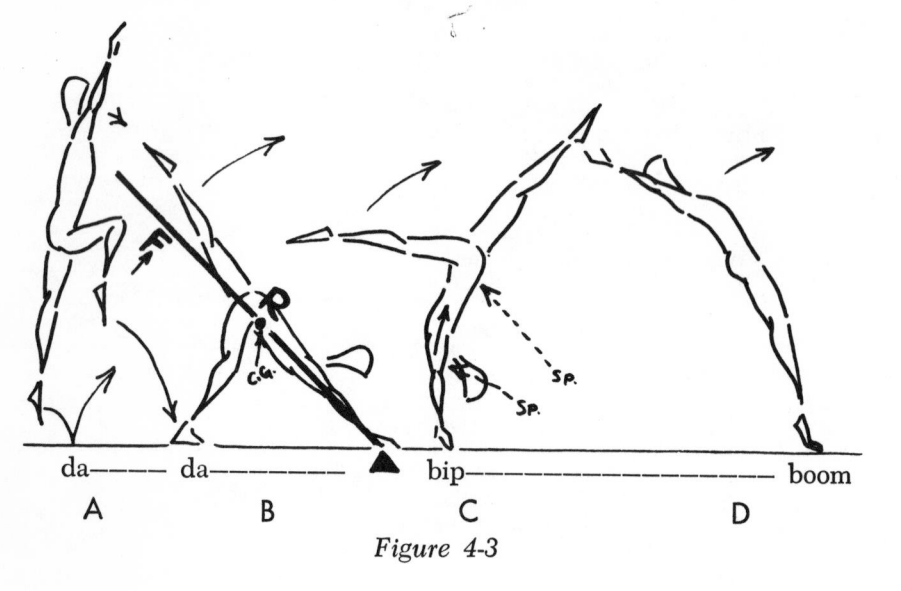

da——— da——————— bip————————————— boom

A   B   C   D

Figure 4-3

The handspring forward is really a vault over floor space and is very similar to the handspring vault in the index in Chapter 3. The body is in the air momentarily between (C) and (D).

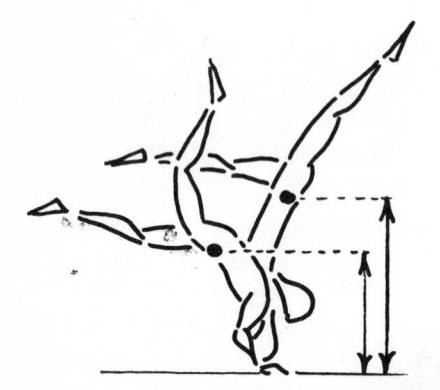

Figure 4-4—Poor and proper positions showing relative heights of C.G.

As in all tumbling movements, a high C. G. is important in the handspring. If your P-A can assist you as shown by the dotted arrows in (C), height can be maintained during the learning stages at proper levels. A good push-off will also raise the C. G.

Some of the easier, related movements found in the handspring are:

1. A momentary handstand (hand support) position.
2. A skip step (Just being completed at A).
3. Backbending is involved and it occurs dynamically.
4. There are moving splits.
5. There is kipping action.

The rhythmical sound you might hear "live" or in imagination is similar to da—— da————— bip ———————————— boom. The da —— da is the the final portion of the skip step; hand placement is "bip" and the landing is "boom."

The explosive part is the kipping action of the right leg from (C) to (D). It explodes to catch up with the leading leg.

First attempts at a handspring can result in unpleasant landings. The P-A should be well prepared to protect the back and hips by pushing as shown.

Dynamic back flexibility plays a role in performance. Notice that the landing of the handspring (D) and the landings shown for the headspring and neckspring (Figures 4-5 and 4-6) are also made with the back hollow. If you have a stiff back this kind of landing will be difficult.

What about leverage? In (B) the body itself is a second class (wheelbarrow) lever device. The hands are at the fulcrum. The dot representing C. G. is the theoretical resistance (R). The force results from the skip step

Figure 4-5   Figure 4-6

speed and a good kick. The force applied as shown results in a forward-upward rotation around the hands, but once the body is in the air the body rotates around the C. G.

Kipping action is more apparent in the close relatives of the handspring shown in Figures 4-5 and 4-6. Since these are ordinarily done without a run, power is generated by a tight piking action (shown in black) which cocks the body for the kip. The explosive action is not as subtle in these movements as it is in the handspring. Since the body is generally lower than in the handspring, more back flexibility is demanded for a good performance.

Your P-A accomplishes two major objectives by assisting performance at the spots marked "Sp." As he pushes and lifts, he reinforces the needed hollow back action and helps raise the C. G.

Let us design a progression for the handspring. We have already mentioned the related movements which are derived in part from Figure 4-3. Remember that part of your progression (the first part) must always be the development of prerequisite physical attributes. In a handspring, hamstring stretch, splits action and hand-supported activity must be the primary elements. You must know how to do a skip step. All your early kip lessons must be well done since kipping is the central theme.

1. Master all prerequisites including a skip step. The skip step must, in in addition, be done exactly where you want it. If not, your P-A will have to guess at the spot and may not be able to help you.
2. Basic kipping action.
3. Kip to a bridge.
4. Roll forward (very slowly) to the black position shown in Figure 4-6 and kip to a bridge. (A bridge is shown in Figure 1-12, the middle figure.)
5. Neckspring with P-A to stand (Figure 4-6).
6. Solo neckspring.
7. Headspring with P-A to stand (Figure 4-5).
8. Solo headspring.
9. Handspring with P-A to feet. This may be preceded by kick-ups without a skip step to learn the action of the leading leg. The P-A catches the leg and simply pushes it back down, preventing you from turning over. Handstands to bridge may also be practiced with a P-A.
10. Solo handspring forward.

Cultivating patience, knowing your strengths and weaknesses and having the intelligence to apply a logical approach will result in good gymnastics. "If you are not ready for it, don't do it," is a good philosophy. There are thousands of challenges that *are* appropriate and fun to do no matter what your level of performance is.

5

Where to Find
Additional Information

If you read all the following books, you will be exposed to the next best source of information. Your best source of information and guidance is the gymnastic specialist, and you are fortunate if such a person is available in your community.

DYSON, GEOFFREY, *The Mechanics of Athletics* 4th ed., London: University of London Press, Ltd., 1967 (a mechanical analysis; excellent material on twisting).

KUNZLE, GEORGE, *Olympic Gymnastics—Horizontal Bar,* London: Barrie and Rockliff, 1957 (best book on horizontal bar).

———, *Olympic Gymnastics—Parallel Bars,* London: Barrie and Rockliff, 1964 (best book on parallel bars).

———, *Olympic Gymnastics—Pommel Horse,* London: Barrie and Rockliff, 1960 (excellent for the side horse).

LAY, GUILIO, *La Tecnique des Sautes—Voltiges.* Write directly to the author, via F. Buontalenti, 8, Prato, Italy, published in 1952 in French and Italian but is so well illustrated that English readers will benefit (best book on vaulting).

MAULDON, E. and J. LAYSON, *Teaching Gymnastics,* London: Macdonald and Evans, Ltd., 1965 (a theoretical approach to movement education).

The Modern Gymnast, official publication of the United States Gymnastic Federation, $5.00 per year, P. O. Box 611, Santa Monica, California 90406 (best magazine available; current events and instructional).

MONROE, A. D., *Pure and Applied Gymnastics* 2nd ed., London: Edward Arnold, Ltd., 1963 (history and development of gymnastics).

SZYPULA, GEORGE, *Tumbling and Balancing for All* 2nd ed., Dubuque, Iowa: Wm. C. Brown Company Publishers, 1968 (best advice on tumbling).

TONRY, DON, *The Side Horse,* Cedar Rapids, Iowa: Nissen Corp., 1966 (excellent for the side horse).

There is no specialized book on the rings.

You may wonder about the fact that the author has included so many English texts. The reason is that there are no comparable books printed in the United States. If you were fluent in German, we could recommend a host of current books which go beyond our list. If you read German, write the Wilhelm-Limpert Verlag, Frankfurt-Main, (Falkensteiner Str. 1) in Germany which is one of the better gymnastic publishing houses.

English publications may be procured through Ling House, 10 Nottingham Place, London, W. 1.

The United States Gymnastic Federation (P. O. Box 4699, Tucson, Arizona) is another excellent source of information. This growing organization is assuming more and more of the burden for gymnastic programming in the United States and its general structure parallels gymnastic federations of other countries which assume the functions of training and competition in all aspects of the activity.

Our final suggestion is that you contact Mr. Glenn Sundby, Editor of *The Modern Gymnast,* P.O. Box 611, Santa Monica, California 90406, who is known the world over as a humble, dedicated promotor of the activity so briefly presented in these pages. If he doesn't know the answer, he will know someone who does.

Index